# What Every Family Needs

## WHATEVER HAPPENED TO MOM, DAD & THE KIDS?

### Carl Brecheen
### &
### Paul Faulkner

GOSPEL
ADVOCATE
PUBLISHERS

NASHVILLE, TENN

Published by Gospel Advocate Company
P.O. Box 150, Nashville, TN  37202
1-800-251-8446

ISBN 0-89225-424-6

# Contents

# The Trouble With Us Is Me

— Self

## Chapter 1

Selfishness is the greatest single enemy of a happy marriage. Selfishness is the root of all other sins. When *I* am at the center of my world, I am out of place and my world is out of balance. The tremors that follow will not stop until they have destroyed something — my marriage, my job, my sanity.

Self-concern is easy to spot. It is when I ask my wife what tv program she wants to watch, but I watch the one I want to see. Selfishness is easy to see in phrases such as, "I'll show you. . . . " It is when I reply, "In a little while . . . " after my children ask me to help them with a project or homework. Selfishness reveals itself in my anger and impatience, and it is really evident when I raise my voice or "cloud up and storm." I operate on pure self-concern when I refuse to get inside the feelings of those who live with me and hurt for their skinned knees or bruised egos.

Selfishness is a natural sin. It comes easy. Remember when you wanted to pitch at the scrub base-

5

ball game, but they wouldn't let you? And how you got furious and stalked off the field, taking your ball — the only one? Selfishness is when I pout or sulk when things don't work out my way.

Selfishness is when my wife suggests that I might be part of the problem, but I deny it or quickly place the blame on someone else instead of honestly evaluating my position. It is *damnable* selfishness when I lie, cheat, steal, or risk another individual to cover my mistakes.

We try our best to hide self-interest. In twenty-five years of ministry, I don't think I have ever heard anyone confess blatant selfishness. We keep it covered like the worn spot in our living room carpet. At least we *think* we keep it covered.

Selfishness pops up in the most unexpected places — like the time my wife found her scarf underneath the car with oil smears on it. Obviously, it had been used to check the oil, but no one knew how the scarf wrapped itself around the dip stick. Then, there was the glass that broke itself in the sink and the flour that jumped out of the pantry onto the floor. Obviously, someone else did it just to get me in trouble.

## It's Mine

Sometimes I hide my personal interests behind my *rights*. That's like the man who came to Jesus upset because he didn't feel his brother had been fair with him in dividing their inheritance. He felt his rights had been violated. Jesus knew it was best not to argue with the man because people are only interested in their own rights.

Jesus made a simple statement to end the conversation and then proceeded to address the root problem — selfish materialism. In Luke 12:15, he said, "Take heed, and beware of all covetousness; for a

6

man's life does not consist in the abundance of his possessions."

Then, Jesus told the parable of the rich farmer. The farmer was so wealthy he couldn't spend it all, so he selfishly said, ". . . I will pull down my barns, and build larger ones. . . ." God said, "Fool! This night your soul is required of you; and the things you have prepared, whose will they be?" (Luke 12:20). That is what happens to the man who is consumed by self-concern.

Satan's first attempt at temptation was successful. He tempted Eve in the garden, and she believed that if she would eat the forbidden fruit she would "be like God—knowing good and evil" (Gen. 3:1-16). To put it bluntly, she elected to take God's position. Satan tempts us the same way today through three aspects of self-centeredness mentioned in 1 John 2:15-16: "the lust of the flesh" (I want it.), "the lust of the eyes" (It is so pretty.), "and the pride of life" (It will make me intelligent.). Pride and lust are forms of selfishness. They have always been Satan's most effective tools.

## A Case of Vertigo

Marriage would be more satisfying if man's nature was inherently good. But, if that is true, why do we make such a mess of things? Robert Nye wrote:

> How do we get off the track of things so that we now raise generation after generation of inadequately functioning individuals? What is the explanation when an apparently highly indulged and freely raised child turns out to be a selfish, manipulative, and generally maladjusted adult? What firm evidence is there for an innate mechanism that helps us make the right choices?[1]

7

David Roberts agrees:

But all men are egocentric at the core. The proper law of human nature is that it shall fulfill itself through dependence upon and harmony with the will of God. But the law of man's *fallen* nature is that he shall strive to make himself the center of the universe. Since he is unsuited to be that, he suffers from the strife and insecurity which attend his efforts to carry through an impossible project. He is driven to seek security by trying to reach self-sufficiency; but he is unable to reach genuine beatitude so long as he fails to center his life in God, whose nature is love.[2]

My human effort alone can not unbend my distorted nature. It takes supernatural power, and Jesus gives me this new nature.

---

## "Theology and history tell us that man has a bad case of vertigo."

---

Theology and history tell us that man has a bad case of *vertigo*. Most of the time, what we think and feel is right really isn't. In fact, we often make wise decisions by determining first what we think is right, then reversing it.

It is like a man caught in a tide carrying him out to sea. The obvious thing to do is swim hard for shore. The reverse — relax, stay afloat, and let the tide carry you — seems quite illogical. Regardless of how unreasonable it sounds, it's the best thing to do.

Once man focused intently on God. But sin distorted his perception and created spiritual vertigo. Through the blood of Jesus, God urges us to accept the divine life again. This requires us to give up our native instinct. Vertigo says that's wrong. We *feel* as

8

though we are giving up something that rightfully belongs to us. Satan makes us think Christ is marching us into bondage, when in reality Christ is restoring us to our original state of glory.

## The Death Principle

Every Christian religion professes, in one form or another, two basic doctrines: baptism, which initiates the Christian into the church; and the Lord's Supper, which memorializes the crucified Savior. Both of these are based on the "death principle," the center of the gospel message.

Paul draws a parallel between Christ's death-burial-resurrection and baptism (Rom. 6:1-17). In baptism, I allow God to dethrone me; and by faith, I allow Christ to become the center of my life. As Christ was buried in the tomb, so I am buried "with him" in baptism. As Christ was raised from the tomb in a new body, so I am raised from the water/grave of baptism to a "newness of life" (Rom. 6:4) to be a "new creation" (2 Cor. 5:17).

In Argentina some Christians baptize with this formula: "I *kill* you in the name of the Father and the Son and the Holy Spirit." As Juan Carlos Ortiz said:

> In baptism, it is more than the tobacco, the drinking and the gambling that stay under the water. It is self. People must understand that. When they come up out of the water, they leave themselves behind. It is a totally new self which now begins to live a life of obedience.[3]

When the Christians' theology in Rome became too lenient, Paul corrected them by reminding them of their death-burial-resurrection. In Romans 6:1-17, he mentions some form of the word death fifteen times.

9

In baptism, I deposit myself into the Lord's account. I can write no more checks on myself because I'm bankrupt. I can no longer brag about anything I have done. Like Paul, I can only boast about Christ and him crucified (Gal. 6:14). Baptism is the picture of absolute helplessness and surrender in the face of absolute love. Pride is just the opposite. It brags and struts in a hundred subtle and not so subtle ways.

It is a paradox, but true: I must die to live. As Christ died to fulfill God's purpose, I must die to fulfill Christ's purpose for me (2 Cor. 5:14-17). This death is not my loss — it is my victory. God has replaced my self-interest with his Spirit (Acts 5:32). His power enables me to triumph over desires of the flesh. I am no longer enslaved; I am free, alive, and victorious.

## Surrendered Rights

As I commit sin, I become a slave of Satan (John 8:34). And slaves don't have rights; they cannot free themselves. Like flies caught on sticky paper, they will die unless an outsider frees them. The only outsider capable of saving me from sin is Jesus. When I accept his blood to cover my sins, I am free.

I am still a slave, but now I am a slave to Christ. You say, "I don't want to be a slave to anybody!" Do you realize there are only two masters — Satan and Christ? And since "No one can serve two masters . . ." (Matt. 6:24), you must choose one.

The concept of absolute freedom is a satanic trick. Satan allows us to think we are "absolutely free," but we are slaves to self. We make ourselves lord by dethroning God and practicing idolatry. We serve self, not God. Families and marriages are happier when their members serve the right master.

A dead man has no resentments. My resentments die as my "rights" die because resentments are caused when rights are violated. If my rights are no longer mine, then my resentments are no longer mine — vengeance belongs to the Lord (Heb. 10:30).

Jesus received an unjust trial. He was mocked, ridiculed, spit upon, and deserted. He had a right to be resentful and bitter, but the words he uttered on the cross had no rancor: ". . . forgive them; for they know not what they do" (Luke 23:34). Stephen and Paul had opportunities to resent unjust treatment (Acts 7:57; 2 Tim. 4:16), but neither responded with resentment because they had buried self with Christ.

---

## "Resentments are caused when rights are violated."

---

Jesus taught this "death principle" during the three years he trained the twelve. At least seven of his parables and much of his teaching cautioned against selfish idolatry. But the disciples were as slow to learn the death principle as we are. James and John tried to get an advantage over the other ten by requesting special places of prominence when Jesus came into his kingdom. When news of this request leaked out to the others, they were "indignant at the two brothers" (Matt. 20:24). Jesus became aware of the agitation and called the twelve together. He suggested that they were acting like worldly people who love to be exalted to high positions so they can control others. In Jesus' kingdom it will be just the opposite. If you want to be right at the top, you must serve like a slave. Your attitude must be like his, for he, "as the Son of man came not to be served but to give his life as a ransom for many" (Matt. 20:28).

11

## Washing Family Feet

One would think the disciples would never forget the death principle, but they did. Jesus later gave them an example and final charge they were never to forget.

As the twelve came up the stairs to the upper room to meet their Lord for the Passover meal, the aroma of the meal appealed to their appetites. The custom was for someone, usually a slave, to wash the feet of the arriving guests. Yet, it wasn't just a custom; it was a necessity because of the unsanitary condition of the streets. Another custom of the East was to recline on one side and eat off of a low table or carpet, with one's feet near the face of another as they formed a semicircle.

Yet, as the Passover meal began, no feet had been washed. No one had offered to wash feet; none had washed his own feet; nor had one even offered to wash Jesus' feet. No one, except Jesus, was willing to be a servant. Peter in outrage said, "Lord do you wash my feet? . . . You shall never wash my feet" (John 13:6-8). Peter must have been humiliated as he watched Jesus wash his feet. It is hard to imagine any of the disciples continuing to eat as they waited for their Lord and Master to wash their feet. Then, in John 13:13-17, Jesus said:

> You call me Teacher and Lord; and you are right, for so I am. If I then, your Lord and Teacher, have washed your feet, you also ought to wash one another's feet. For I have given you an example, that you also should do as I have done to you . . . a servant is not greater than his master. . . . If you know these things, blessed are you if you do them.

To be a husband or wife according to God's plan means servanthood. What was true for Jesus and his disciples is true for the husband and wife (Eph. 5:21-33).

I must give up resentment of doing things beneath my dignity. When I see my wife behind in her work — the dishes need washing, the tub needs cleaning, the trash needs carrying out — I do it. It wasn't Jesus' job to wash feet, but it was not humiliating to him. He did not resent it. Jesus modeled what he called his disciples to do.

## Why "My Way" Will Not Work

### 1. My Way Clouds Judgment.

As King Saul went to battle the Amalekites, he was instructed by God's prophet Samuel to "utterly destroy all that they have; . . . man and woman . . . ox and sheep, camel and ass" (1 Sam. 15:3). But Saul used his own judgment and returned from the battle with a huge surplus of loot. God sent Samuel to meet Saul to challenge his disobedient action. Saul defended himself and said, "I have performed the commandment of the Lord" (1 Sam. 15:13).

Self dominated the mind of Saul and clouded his judgment — perhaps even his memory.

Prejudice blinded the judgment of the Jewish Sanhedrin when it made the decision to crucify Jesus. The council members were afraid that their place and nation would be destroyed (John 11:48).

### 2. My Way Is Never Satisfied.

Selfishness is never satisfied. The more it gets, the more it wants. King Solomon began his reign as a man of God, full of wisdom and splendor. Unfortunately, he watered down his faithfulness to God with self-serving allegiances: many wives and concubines, gold, and riches — much of which came from heavy taxation of his people.

Toward the end of his life Solomon looked back

on his accumulated wealth and said, "Vanity of vanties....All is vanity" (Eccles. 1:2-3). He had quenched every physical appetite, but it was all in vain. Howard Hughes and John Paul Getty did the same in this generation. Self is a good servant, but as a master it is a tyrant. Selfishness is never satisfied until it completely consumes.

### 3. My Way Doesn't Pay, It Costs.

King David allowed his lust for a woman to lead him to adultery. His cover-up tactics didn't work, so he killed her innocent husband (2 Sam. 11). David later repented of this sin that was ever before him (Ps. 51). But the effect of his sin spread to his children and the whole nation of Israel.

Anyone who remains very close to a self-centered person will have to bear some of the consequences of his actions, even though they are innocent. That is the nature of the disease. This can be seen in a family where the wife and children pay the price for the husband's reputation of adultery and bad debts.

### 4. My Way Doesn't Work In The Long Run.

Earth life is only a prelude to eternal life. When we treat life on this earth as the total package, we misunderstand and misappropriate the gift of life. It is like a caterpillar that sells its right to become a butterfly for one stomach full of leaves. The young prodigal son in Luke 15: 11-24 was shortsighted. He didn't investigate the results of his self-indulgence. Only the body comes to an end when a person dies, and it will be resurrected in the judgment day.

### 5. My Way Gets in God's Way.

". . . It is not in man who walks to direct his steps" (Jer. 10:23). Often what I think is a stepping stone is a stumbling block in God's view. Moses wanted to deliver the Israelites prematurely, but it didn't work. He became angry, disillusioned, and un-cooperative, even when God told him it was the proper time to deliver Israel (Exod. 3-4). "There is a way that seems right to a man, but its end is the way to death" (Prov. 14:12).

### 6. My Way Dissipates Me.

To live according to the "gospel of me" spells disaster. I know that I am not God, but sometimes to keep up my image, I act like it.

Saul enthroned himself as king. He continually rejected overtures of God's mercy and moved on — headstrong, resulting in insanity and madness (1 Sam. 18). Judas enthroned himself and committed suicide. Hitler followed the same pattern.

To enthrone *self* is a form of mental suicide. To be exalted, one must become the "slave of all" (Mark 10:43-44). It is just the reverse of what the natural man thinks.

### 7. My Way Stunts Growth.

When I do everything my way, I have no opportunity to learn from others. I am doomed to commit the same mistakes over and over because I won't listen to or learn from others. My horizons are too narrow.

### 8. My Way Allows No Freedom.

My way is undisciplined. It is a long line of urges, wants, and desires. Selfishness is not found around freedom. Undisciplined people follow the path of least resistance. The person who does only what he wants never completes difficult jobs. He is always behind and in debt.

Freedom comes through self-denial. No person is free from financial trouble if he uses charge cards unwisely. ". . . God did not give us a spirit of timidity but a spirit of power and love and self control" (2 Tim. 1:7).

### 9. My Way Causes Dissension.

Self-seekers are just that — seekers. Their attitude is "me first."

The Corinthian church was a quarreling family (1 Cor. 1;4; 12-14). Men were making names for themselves, not for God. They were puffed up, full of pride, and not living according to scripture. Paul makes it plain that God gives us gifts and abilities; they are not earned (1 Cor. 4:7).

Paul pleads for the maturity which comes by understanding that we have no reason to boast, for "grace was given to each of us according to the measure of Christ's gift" (Eph. 4:7). How can I boast of my accomplishments when I am "not my own" (1 Cor. 6:19)? I was bought with Christ's blood. How can I be selfish when everything I have of value is a gift?

James sums it up: "For where jealousy and selfish ambition exist, there will be disorder and every vile practice" (James 3:16).

### 10. My Way Separates Me From God.

There is room for only one throne in my heart. It will be occupied by God or self. When I enthrone myself, I dethrone God. "No one can serve two masters; for either he will hate the one and love the other, or he will be devoted to the one and despise the other. You cannot serve God and mammon" (Matt. 6:24).

## Drawing On The Power

Selfishness and immaturity can destroy a home. Before there can be a permanent cure for this problem, the individuals in the home must first be examined. *I* must get the selfish part of *me* out of the way so *we* can grow. Jesus said in Matthew 7:4-5 that I must first get the beam out of my own eye, so I can see clearly to get the mote out of yours. How could there be anything more practical than that?

If a brick house is beginning to crack, it is useless to reset the bricks until the foundation is repaired. So it is with a family. If husband and wife are fighting and the children are rebellious, going to a sex seminar will do no good. The foundation must be repaired.

Do the two principal characters in the home have strong Christian values? Are they mature, selfless, and disciplined? There is no problem too big to overcome in a marriage if a foundation of personal integrity is found in Mom and Dad. Builders can make an unstable house look pretty for awhile, but eventually a house without a strong foundation will fall (Matt. 7:24ff).

Here are six steps that help draw on the power of God to defeat self-centeredness.

1. Be *humble* enough to admit that self-centeredness is sin (Gal. 2:20; Matt. 6:24). Do not rationalize, play selfishness down, or project it on circumstances or others.

2. Rely by *faith* on God to help me live beyond my self-interest (John 8:24).

3. *Turn* my life from serving self to serving others. When I serve others, I am pointed in the right direction. In the Bible, demonstrated selflessness is called repentance (Luke 13:3).

4. *Confirm* to myself and others that I am willing to kill the old life and be resurrected to a new life in Christ. This is illustrated by the concept of baptism (Rom. 6:3; Gal. 3:27; Acts 2:38).

5. *Restore* the peace destroyed by my selfishness. Make apologies, repair the damage, and accept forgiveness if I cannot repay the damage (Matt. 5:23-26).

6. *Enjoy* the gifts of God in Christ. He has promised the gift of the Holy Spirit in our life (Acts 5:32). Therein is power, a source of energy when I fail, and

new power in prayer (Rom. 8:26-27).

O Divine Master, grant that I may not so much
seek
To be consoled as to console;
To be understood as to understand;
To be loved as to love;
For it is in giving that we receive;
It is in pardoning that we are pardoned;
It is in dying that we are born to eternal life.
(See John 3:5.)

Francis of Assisi

---

[1]Nye, Robert, *Three Views Of Man* (Monterey: Brooks & Cole, 1975), pp. 134, 135.

[2]Roberts, David E., *Psychotherapy and A Christian View Of Man,* pp. 85-86.

[3]Ortiz, Juan Carlos, *Disciple* (Carol Stream: Creation House, 1975), p. 53.

# I Need Your Help

## – Husbands

### Chapter 2

Recent research has concluded that "the personality and background of the husband, not the wife, were the important factors in the success of a marriage. "[1]

Another writer said, "Studies of delinquency repeatedly indicate that fathers are more influential than mothers in the development of delinquent behavior in their children."[2]

Two sociologists from the University of Southern California studied 2,004 blue-collar families in Los Angeles for four years and concluded that "if the father attends church regularly, the children will be more likely to attend regularly — *regardless of the mother's attendance record.*"[3]

Husbands, before you read this chapter, check the items below that apply to you (leave the others blank). It will help you get a better insight into your practice of being a husband or a father.

1. ( ) You usually take work home at night.
2. ( ) You usually are away from home ten hours or more a day.
3. ( ) Your wife has not been on a trip with you in three years.
4. ( ) Most of your social relationships are related to your work.
5. ( ) Your family dinner is often interrupted (by phone calls or whatever).
6. ( ) Your wife has little understanding of the inside details of your work.
7. ( ) You find it hard to kiss your wife with meaning without it leading to the bedroom.
8. ( ) Nagging, bickering, and picking are general occurrences at your home.
9. ( ) Housework is beneath your dignity.
10. ( ) Financially, you are somewhat more liberal with yourself than with your wife.
11. ( ) You haven't had a date with your wife in two weeks.
12. ( ) You find it hard to say "I love you" and mean it every day.
13. ( ) Your children tend to annoy you.
14. ( ) You ask which tv program she would like to see; then, you watch the one you prefer.
15. ( ) You prefer to watch tv than talk with your wife.
16. ( ) Your wife has caught you in little lies, which you have tried to wiggle out of.
17. ( ) When wrong, you find it hard to admit.
18. ( ) You neglect to phone in when late for dinner.
19. ( ) You have three or more years of formal education than your wife has.
20. ( ) Your wife has no additional formal education since you were married.

21. (   ) You dislike detail and methodical attitudes.
22. (   ) You dislike saving money.
23. (   ) It is impossible for you to account for where most of your money goes each month.
24. (   ) You are inclined to buy things on impulse and then have trouble paying your bills.
25. (   ) You find it difficult to spend time examining your purpose in life. (Who am I? Why am I here? Where am I going?)
26. (   ) Your prime interests center more around things than people.
27. (   ) You have had two fights in the last two weeks.
28. (   ) You haven't had a fight in two years.
29. (   ) You often express irreligious attitudes.
30. (   ) You are inclined to be moody.
31. (   ) You neglect to kiss your wife every morning when leaving.
32. (   ) You are more inclined to be radical in sex, morals, and politics.

If you checked very many of the above statements you need to read on — this chapter is for you. If you checked none of the above statements, you are unreal. Please hand the book to your wife and see how *she* scores you.

The first eighteen items are complaints made by wives about unsatisfactory husbands. Items 19-32 are characteristics of unsatisfactory husbands, as discovered by researchers. The fewer items you checked, the better husband you should be.

In contrast to that test, Lewis Terman presents a list of characteristics of "happily married men."[4] You are an ideal husband if you can check *all* of the following:

1. ( ) Have even and stable emotional tone.
2. ( ) Are cooperative.
3. ( ) Show attitude toward women that reflects equalitarian ideals.
4. ( ) Have benevolent attitude toward inferiors and the underprivileged.
5. ( ) Tend to be unselfconscious and somewhat extroverted.
6. ( ) Show superior initiative.
7. ( ) Have greater tendency to take responsibility.
8. ( ) Show greater willingness to give close attention to detail.
9. ( ) Like methodical procedures and methodical people.
10. ( ) Are saving and cautious in money matters.
11. ( ) Hold conservative attitudes.
12. ( ) Have favorable attitude toward religion.
13. ( ) Strongly uphold the sex mores and other social conventions.

## Common Complaints From Women About Their Husbands

I have asked many wives this question: "If your husband would agree to give you *anything* you would ask of him, what *one* thing would you ask for?" Here are some of the answers:

"More time."

"More understanding."

"Stronger leadership."

"Affection in public."

"If he could just teach me like he teaches others" (a preacher's wife).

"That he wouldn't think he had all the answers."

"That he doesn't always have to give an answer."

"Be more forgiving."

"I would like him to pass the salt to me first."
(They had been married thirty-four years.)

"I would like for him to fix the car lights."

"A weekly allowance and not have to give an account for what I do with it."

"Listen to me more instead of making me feel like I'm talking to a hollow tree."

"For him to like me fat and gray."

"To care more about my feelings when those feelings are not the same as his own."

"Pay more compliments and notice me more."

"Accept me as I am."

"Be more forgiving." (They had been married thirty-eight years.)

"Need me more."

Few wives asked for what most husbands thought they wanted. None asked for prestige, wealth, or power. Most wives asked for little things, personal things, courtesies, consideration, love, and time.

Hopefully, an understanding of what wives *really* want will help take pressure off husbands and will free them to really enjoy their wives and families. Here are seven common complaints I hear from wives about their husbands:

1. **Selfishness.** This is always near the top of the list. Wives are generally more yielding than husbands. They resent it when the husband uses the woman's generosity for his own benefit. For example, the wife may say, "I don't really care where we eat, you choose." If the husband always chooses *his* favorite eating spot, that is selfish. Sometimes his choice should be *her* favorite spot — because he *wants* to please *her.*

It really hurt me when I received this letter from a lady:

I realize how much I need emotional support,

23

and my husband can't give it to me. It's eating me up inside. I know what the Bible says about divorce and remarriage, but I don't believe I can live the rest of my life this unhappy. I'm thirty-one.

Her husband *can* give her emotional support, but *won't*. He is insensitive to her needs. If he would only forget himself and seek to fulfill her emotional needs, he would make both of them happy.

2. **Pride (stubbornness).** Many wives feel their husbands seldom yield. Even when proven wrong, many husbands rationalize and try to justify a false cause. Is it because it is "unmanly" to yield to a woman? Or is it perhaps that the home is the only place a husband can successfully resist? Researcher Berthold Berg contends that "consistent with other investigations, the father was viewed as the most resistant along a number of dimensions."[5] "Most resistant" is a nice word for stubborn.

---

### *"Almost twice as many wives go for marriage counseling as husbands."*

---

Pride causes husbands to refuse professional, medical, and marital help. Almost twice as many wives go for marriage counseling as husbands. Even when husbands admit their marriage is in jeopardy, they frequently retort, "We don't have to go to a counselor. We can work it out by ourselves." And they probably can if they really work at it. But usually they won't, so matters get worse. If husbands were less "resistant," counselors could get to the root of the marital problems much sooner.

Successful men hate to admit failure. If a man plans to quit smoking or drinking, he usually does not announce it until he can see that he is reaching his goal. If he publicly announces his intention to quit and then doesn't, he runs the risk of being ridiculed. And few men can take that.

The basic neurosis of a man is to have tried and failed. A wise woman will allow an escape hole for a man's ego to slip through when things get rough. Often a man appears to be stubborn when really he is just trying to "save face."

Women also complain that husbands do not take enough pride in their personal hygiene and physical appearance. A clean, good-smelling, neatly-dressed husband is a delight to a woman. One wife complained, "My husband is a hard-working day laborer, who bathes only about twice a month." Seldom do men realize how repulsive this is to women.

**3. Won't Read.** "My husband can read well enough, but won't," some wives complain. What they *do* read is limited — usually only the local paper (front page, sports, and comics, in reverse order). Most men are not aware of events that are of interest to their wives.

Publishers know this. That is why they seldom publish books exclusively for men. Intelligent, well-written women's magazines flourish. Few men's magazines exist that are not filled with lewd pictures of women — a sad commentary on the "reading" interest of men. (A few good books are listed at the end of this chapter. I hope every man will read at least two.)

I require couples I counsel to "double read" a book to multiply the effectiveness of reading. Both husband and wife mark or underline with a different colored pen the parts of the book (s)he identifies with. As they read and mark, each reads the author's comments and the parts of the book underlined by the other. You will be pleasantly surprised to find aspects of your partner's personality you never knew before. Your relationship will be enriched when your spouse writes "this is me" or "this is exactly how I feel" in the margin. It's like reading two books at once. (I hope you are double reading *this* book.)

4. **Lack of Common Courtesy (manners).** A woman loves the kind of attention she received during courtship. When a woman marries, she assumes that the courtship will continue. But husbands often forget the simple things that make a wife feel special. He thinks that courtship is a "stage" that passes with time. But little things make a woman's life more enjoyable: calling her sweetheart (or any special name), reminding her of how much she is needed, opening doors for her, bringing her little gifts, mailing her love notes or cards, or love and kindness given her in daily conversations and decisions. She doesn't want to *ask* for these things. She wants them to come from his heart. Women need to be needed.

5. **Lack of Insight and Energy.** Too many husbands think their job is over when they walk out of the office. A woman thinks it is only right (especially when she also works out of the home) that her husband put equal amounts of creative thought and energy into the daily development of the home and children (physically, intellectually, *and spiritually*).

Professor Walters notes that "studies of delinquency repeatedly indicate that fathers are more influential than mothers in the development of delinquent behavior in their children."[6] This may be due to the husband's failure to put his insight and energies into creating a Christian home. The many pressures on the family from without and within the home increase the need for parents to combine their efforts to create a Christian atmosphere.

6. **Lack of Priorities.** I often hear: "My husband is

working himself to death to provide for our family, but we would really prefer to live on less and have him home more." God-fearing wives do not give top priority to the "company," jobs, promotions, things, or money. Uprooting a family for a $500 or $1,000 raise may not be putting God and the family first.

Mothers feel stifled and inadequate when they have to teach children about God with no help from the father. Often the child's image of God comes directly from the child's image of his father. When the husband does not assume the leadership role in the family's religion, the whole family suffers.

7. **Lack of Communication.** I saved one of the greatest complaints from wives until last. Women believe most problems in marriage are surmountable "if we could only talk." Because this complaint is so frequently voiced, we have devoted one entire chapter in this book to communication. Husbands would do well to "double read" this chapter.

## The Husband As God Would Have Him

Here are some biblical principles that characterize the Christian husband.

**Provider.** It is taken for granted the husband is to financially and physically sustain the family. From the very beginning God said man would struggle to extract a living from the ground (Gen. 3:17-19). However, the scriptures do not designate the husband as sole provider of financial income (Prov. 31).

There are greater things than money and physical needs that a man must provide his family. God has given the Christian father the responsibility of providing spiritual, intellectual, and emotional leadership — the truly essential needs.

**Leader-Lover.** I have combined these words into one concept because to "lead" without loving is cruel and to "love" without leading is a "cop out" on God's concept of husbanding (Eph. 5:21-33). The husband is the leader, the one to whom the wife must be in subjection (vss. 21-24). However, the context of his leadership is "love as Christ loved the church" (vss. 25-33).

The husband's leadership role in the American home is declining. A survey of 340,000 homes conducted by *Better Homes and Gardens* magazine[7] produced surprising results. Those who participated were asked: "Do you think the dominant role of the husband in the American family is declining in importance?" Seventy-nine percent replied, "Yes," as expected. The unexpected result followed the next question: "Would you consider a decline in the husband's dominance to be good?" *Seventy-one* percent said, "No." Most Americans believe the husband is still more effective as the leader in the home.

---

## "The leader presides at the 'foot' of the table; not the 'head.' "

---

The leadership role is not a coveted role. The person in this position must ultimately take responsibility for *everything* that goes wrong and try to get the family back on target. Like the president of a corporation, he may not always be the person to blame, but he is always the person responsible for getting the train back on the track and moving. He is the one who figures out what's causing the tension, then moves to relieve it.

Neither does the leadership role mean superiority or permit a "tight-fisted dictator." The leader presides at the "foot" of the table, not the "head" (Matt. 20:25-28; John 13:13-17).

According to Dean Merrill, Jesus has created:

a new . . . role: the leader/servant. The chief/ Indian. The honcho/peon. He acknowledged the need for leadership. Jesus was not an anarchist. But neither was he willing to tolerate the all-too-frequent abuses of power. Leadership, he said, is earned, is indeed made possible only by serving.[8]

The Christian leader must cleanse his heart of selfish motives before making decisions. This validates his leadership and makes him followable. He must realize that what authority he has is not really his, for all his authority originates in God. He is expected to be a good steward of God's authority. To serve the Lord is to *serve His family.*

God's definition of love is unique:

```
God ................the source of all authority
so loved ................the degree of his love
that he gave his Son............the cost — the
   only thing he could not make  (John 3:16)
while we were sinners.........our condition:
   the worst possible (Rom. 5:6-8)
```

A worldly husband shows love with things. He gives things to his family or friends when he is pleased with them. A Christian husband gives the most precious thing he has — himself — even when his loved ones are at their worst. This is the highest kind of love, divine love. Anyone can love people when they are lovable. But loving people at their worst is divine.

Love is more of a verb than a noun; it is more of an action than a feeling. R.C. Sproul explains:

> When Paul says, "Love your wives," he is saying, "Be loving toward your wife — treat her as lovely." Do the things that are truly loving things. If a husband doesn't feel romantic toward his wife, that does not mean he can't be loving.

29

Is there any problem that a man could possibly have with his wife that Christ hasn't had with the church? Yet He continues to love her. If one partner refuses to obey his responsibilities and violates his role, that does not relieve the other person from responsibility. God does not say, "Wives be submissive to your husbands when they are loving," or "Husbands love your wives when they are submissive." Two wrongs still don't add up to a right. Retaliation brings no honor to Christ.[9]

Love grows by actions of love and casting yourself in love's direction even when you do not feel loving toward a person. When we reverse the order and act as ugly as we feel, we destroy ourselves as well as others. This well-known saying is true: "It is easier to act yourself into a better way of feeling than to feel yourself into a better way of acting."

Love never forces itself:

The Shulhan Aruka insists that there must be not only consent TO marriage, but, for the dignity of both and the high level of love, there must be consent IN marriage. In Jewish law, the husband's conjugal (sexual) rights do not include that of approaching his wife *without her consent*. He must woo her . . . through the years of married life; only the am-haaretz ("brutal ignoramus") would ever transgress this public prohibition.[10]

**Knows God.** How can a husband be a leader if he doesn't know who he is or where he is going? Only a Christian concept of God provides these answers. An ideal husband has a philosophy that gives meaning and purpose to life. He strives toward definite goals and knows the answer to the inevitable question of every human being: What am I here for? If he accepts the humanist philosophy that "this world is all there is," his leadership is drastically affected. It doesn't take much leadership if we are not going anywhere.

The Christian philosophy gives meaning and purpose to living, makes sense, provides direction and values that are sound, and, as a consequence, gives stability to the home. The instability of many homes today is directly related to the instability of many husbands.

**Honors the Wife.** "Likewise you husbands, live considerately with your wives, bestowing *honor* on the woman as the weaker sex, . . ." (1 Pet. 3:7). A wife is created in the image of God (Gen. 1:27). Therefore, she is to be honored by her husband. Honor comes from the heart of a man when he respects God's opinion of his wife's value. Adam and Abraham both failed to honor their wives as they should and were reprimanded (Gen. 3:12; 12:11-19).

The mind of the husband must reserve a place of honor for her permanently in his life because she is Christ's and ONE with the husband. If a father dishonors the wife, the children will also dishonor her. She not only loses influence with the children, but her self-esteem suffers.

To dishonor the wife hinders prayer life because God will not hear a husband who dishonors his wife: ". . . bestowing honor on the woman . . . since you are joint heirs of the grace of life, in order that your prayers may not be hindered" (1 Pet. 3:7). A husband who does not honor his wife as a gift from God cuts himself off from God.

To honor her is to give her dignity.

The Latin equivalent of the Greek word for glory is "dignitas." When the New Testament speaks of the church's glory, it is speaking of its dignity. By analogy, the husband is called to give himself to the purpose of establishing his wife in the fullness of dignity. When he uses his authority to destroy his wife's dignity, he becomes the direct antithesis of Christ. He mirrors not Christ, but the Antichrist.[11]

**Knows the Family.** "Likewise you husbands, live *considerately* with your wives," (1 Pet. 3:7). There is no way the president of a corporation can effectively lead unless he knows the organization "inside out." The same is true of the family. Husbands can't lead unless they know their wives and children "inside out." Getting to know each one thoroughly takes time and effort. When a child says, "But, Dad, you don't understand," it's time to stop and think.

All of us have certain basic needs. When a need is not fulfilled, we usually substitute something inferior to fill that empty space. If we are rejected by those we want for friends, we will find others less desirable because we need people in our lives.

The father should know the unique needs of each family member, but this is not easy. It may take years; but if a man really wants to know his family, he can learn to become super sensitive to *their* needs by seeing through *their* eyes, feeling through *their* fingertips, and hearing through *their* ears. Techniques to do this can be learned, but techniques are not as important as an honest desire to truly know his family.

**Trainer-Teacher-Enricher-Facilitator.** "Fathers, do not provoke your children to anger, but bring them up in the discipline and instruction of the Lord"

(Eph. 6:4). The father is "head trainer." With knowledge and insight, he will recognize areas of deficiency in each family member. He should then plan a program of enrichment to help each person become a fully-functioning Christian.

Twelve-year-old Beverly may be shy or withdrawn because of being overweight. Her father should watch for insights to learn how she feels and what she thinks. A sensitive father would develop a plan to treat the cause, as well as the symptom (shyness).

Each family member also has special gifts. Dad should search for them until he discovers some unique abilities of each family member, then plan for their enhancement.

A leader's real strength lies in his ability to discover and utilize the resources of those he is leading. The husband's job is to discover, in companionship with the wife, *God's way* for his family without settling for the easy path of stereotyped living.

---

**"A leader's real strength lies in his ability to discover and utilize the resources of those he is leading."**

---

The father usually fails if he doesn't see his family as a unit, an organism, each part functioning to benefit the others. If he allows members of his family to develop into strong individualists, each doing his own thing with little regard for the other, they will work against him. No business executive would allow his organization to develop factions. Also, a father can't lead his family any faster than they are willing or able to follow. He must stay in touch with their feelings about the pace and may have to slow down.

**Example.** Jesus left us an example that we might follow in his steps (1 Pet. 2:21); therefore, the husband must also live an exemplary life. To profess a noble way of life without living it does more harm than good. Whatever dominates a man's daily living speaks louder than what he says. The way a son treats his mother and sisters is probably learned by observing how Dad treats Mom. A father must demonstrate, as well as teach his children, how to love. Children learn to love in the same manner they are loved.

How courteous are you to the family? What do you convey by your tone of voice? Do you use crude language? Is modesty a part of your behavior? Are your remarks about the preacher or public figures in good taste? Do you demonstrate self-control? After you've almost had a wreck, how do you talk about other drivers in the presence of your children? Do you gossip about your neighbors in front of your children? Ask yourself, "Do I want my children to be like I am? Do I lead my children or do I preach *at* them?" Dad must set an example of *being* a servant as Jesus did — including everything from teaching, earning money, and listening patiently to family problems — to doing the dirtiest household task.

**Considerate.** "Husbands, in the same way be considerate as you live with your wives, and treat them with respect . . ." (1 Pet. 3:7, NIV). The word "considerate" implies "understanding, investigative insight, sensitive." Courtesy is "love in trifles" — it shows we care. One lady said, "It is passing the salt to me first."

When people stop being considerate, they start taking each other for granted. Courtesy is keeping a sensitive ear to what the other would like. One lady said, "I would like to be owned. I would like for him to let other people know that he likes me." Another said, "Just be patient with me as I get slower. We have been married thirty-two years, and things are slowing down."

The considerate husband is sensitive to what his wife thinks is romantic. One wife told me about the "date" her husband planned. He slipped out the back door, rang the front door bell, and presented her with a bouquet of flowers. His wife blushed with joy as she retold the story. Consideration is sweet talk, taking her breakfast in bed, opening doors, helping around the house (without being asked), and never forgetting about birthdays, anniversaries, and Mother's Days. Consideration is NOT being critical, being crude, or hurting feelings. Consideration is doing to others what you would have them do to you (Matt. 7:12), thinking ahead to avoid frustrating moments, phoning when you see you are going to be late, calling home in the evenings when you are out of town, picking up after yourself (dishes and clothes), and never inviting company over without the knowledge and consent of your mate.

**A Friend.** Who is your best friend? If your answer is someone other than your wife, it may be a reflection on your marriage. Perhaps the best test of the condition of the relationship between a husband and wife is to determine the extent of their friendship.

Friends enjoy being in the company of each other because they enhance each other, enjoy most of the same things, look out for each other, and do not want the other to be hurt or embarrassed. There are no ulterior motives. They try to "understand" each other; and even when they don't understand, they still believe. Even when they hurt each other, it wasn't on "purpose." They can't stand not to be friends.

**Imperfect.** As a husband, I know I am not perfect. I make many mistakes. I feel incomplete. I need my wife to fill some of the gaps — to complete me. When I act bold and self assured, frequently I am covering inadequacies. A man wants his wife to realize he is imperfect. But he doesn't need to be criticized, especially in public. He needs encouragement to stand up to his God-given task. Maybe he is "on edge" because he is the one in the family who has to cast a "tie-breaking" vote. He often gets the blame when things go wrong, yet sometimes he caused them to go wrong. But even when he is wrong, he needs to know that his wife is standing by his side. Most husbands would reject marriage if they felt that every time they did something wrong their wives were going to "set them straight."

Christian husbands try to be God's men and do his will for their families, continually petitioning for God's help. They know they often falter in wisdom and temperament, and this may make them feel terrible. A man needs assurance that his wife ". . . does him good, and not harm, all the days of her life" (Prov. 31:12), even though he is imperfect. On the other hand, criticism seldom changes a stubborn man. It only verifies his negative self-image, and he often becomes more stubborn.

## Some Suggestions

The following suggestions will work; they have all been tried. Select one or two that you think will work for you and try them. Follow through to completion, and then evaluate their effectiveness. Next, turn back to the list again and select another one or two to work through.

They are simple. Some may seem silly, but every suggestion comes from the life of a couple. Remember, they are of value only when they get beyond this page and into your life.

1. Have a planned date with your spouse every two weeks, and every two months set a "big date" to eat out or go to a show.

2. For husbands: concentrate on your wife's *feelings*. For wives: concentrate on your husband's *thoughts*. *Listen* for them and respond to them; they are the wedges by which you pry open the real person underneath.

3. For husbands: share your appointment book with her. Consult her before you make any appointment that would take you away from her or the children.

4. Together list your joint and individual commitments to things like job, children, retirement, friends, bank loans, church, etc. Then, on a scale from 1 to 10, privately rank each of them. Next, get back together and talk about your "family priorities."

5. For husbands: frequently give her gifts — little, perishable gifts. Wrap each one personally. *Listen* to her so intently that when she hints she would like to have a certain thing (a color of Kleenex, for example), she has it — from you.

6. Keep a card in your wallet/purse with your spouse's sizes on it. When you are away from home, shop for something nice. And remember the favorite colors.

7. Ask your partner (perhaps on one of your dates): "What do you think are my gifts from God, my capabilities as a person?" Then, both of you explore how these gifts might be used in the future. To what extent is God calling him/her?

8. Try *NOT* to invest much of your money or self into things that tend to separate you. We tend to follow our investments, so dialogue on and prioritize your *investments*.

9. Consciously reschedule your life in the direc-

tion you want it to go. We tend to allow the *urgent* things to mold us instead of the *important* things.

10. Pray. Make sure you spend time in prayer and meditation, with some of it in partnership prayer with your spouse. It can be the sweetest time of your lives.

11. Share your experiences, your successes, and your failures — *as frequently as they occur.*

12. Use your influence, position, and business skills to help the family.

13. Make small compromises. You don't have to have your way all the time to be happy.

14. Make meaningful use of family time. Quality time is more important than quantity time. When you must be home only a short time, use it effectively.

15. Stop hiding behind alibis; they don't work. The excuse, "I'm doing it for my wife and family," is no cover-up for a father who spends too much time on the job.

16. Schedule time for your family first. This is not "down time" or an expenditure, *it is an investment.*

17. Let yourself be interrupted during your business day by and for the family. Give your children your phone number at work, and encourage them to call you when they need you.

18. If you travel and are away at night, maintain the "conversation" by calling in every night (when possible). Remain in the parenting role when you call in by talking with each family member a few moments.

19. Work for the company part of the time and for the family part of the time. Husbands, tell your wives, "I will work late tonight, but I'll give up my weekend golf date."

20. Don't attempt to buy your children's affection.

Buy personal, rather than expensive, gifts that show you *know* them and their likes and dislikes.

21. Show courtesy. Don't park your manners outside the door. No one has a right to be rude, ill-mannered, or insensitive to others.

---

[1]Dorothy Nevill and Sandra Damico, "The Importance of the Husband to Marital Success," *Human Relations*, p. 485.

[2]Deborah Lang and Rudolf Papenfuhs, "Delinquent Females' Perceptions of their Fathers," *The Family Coordinator* (October 1976), p. 475.

[3]Vern Gengston and Alan Acock, *Youth Letter Magazine* (March 1977), p. 21.

[4]Lewis M. Terman, *Psychological Factors in Marital Happiness*. (The research is old but valid, none the less.)

[5]Berg, Berthold, Rosenblum, Neil, "Fathers in Family Therapy: A Survey of Family Therapists," *Journal of Marriage and Family Counseling* (April 1977), p. 85.

[6]Lang, p. 475.

[7]Meredith Corporation, "A Report on the American Family," *Better Homes and Gardens*. (The 1977 survey showed a significant drop in the percentage. Nevertheless, the majority (55%) of secular America still felt a "decline in the husband's dominance.")

[8]Dean Merrill, *The Husband Book* (Grand Rapids: Zondervan, 1977), p. 27.

[9]R.C. Sproul, *Discovering the Intimate Marriage* (Minneapolis: Bethany Fellowship, Inc., 1975), pp. 76-77.

[10]Hirsch L. Silverman, *Marital Counseling* (Springfield: C.C. Thomas, 1967), p. 276.

[11]Sproul, p. 81.

# I Need Your Love
## — Wives

Chapter 3

Marriage quickly reveals that women are not like men. They don't *look* like men; they don't *act* like men; and they don't even *think* like men.

Husbands often fail to recognize these differences, and so they treat their wives as though they were men. Husbands assume their wives will understand when things don't go right; yet, wives break down in tears at a "simple suggestion." Then, husbands throw up their hands and say, "I don't understand her!"

Generally, communication breaks down because husbands and wives are not sensitive to their unique differences — differences that are innately God-given.

This chapter is written to help promote understanding. It will highlight the unique qualities of a woman and how a wife is distinctive from her husband.

## 1. A wife is a GIFT to her husband.

> ... the Lord God called to man, and said to him, "Where are you?" And he said, "I heard the sound of thee ... I was naked; and I hid myself." He said, "Who told you that you were naked? Have you eaten of the tree of which I commanded you not to eat?" The man said, "The woman *whom thou gavest to be with me,* she gave me fruit of the tree, and I ate.
>
> Genesis 3:9–12

Since the beginning, men have had a tendency to blame their wives or God for their problems.

God gave Eve to Adam as a gift. Precious gifts are not to be abused or flaunted; they are to be treated graciously out of respect for the giver. For a husband to neglect or abuse his wife is to work against God's purpose: "Enjoy life with the wife whom you love ... because that is your portion in life" (Eccles. 9:9).

## 2. A wife is ONE with her husband.

> Then the man said, "This at last is bone of my bones and flesh of my flesh; she shall be called Woman, because she was taken out of Man." Therefore a man leaves his father and his mother and cleaves to his wife, and they become one flesh.
>
> Genesis 2:23, 24

God made man and beast out of the dust of the earth (Gen. 2:7, 19), but he made woman in a special way — out of man. Paul calls attention to this special relationship:

> Even so husbands should love their wives as their own bodies. He who loves his wife loves himself. For no man ever hates his own flesh, but nourishes and cherishes it, ... For this

41

reason a man shall leave his father and mother and be joined to his wife, and the two shall become one flesh.

Ephesians 5:28-31

I should no more consider hurting my wife or cutting her out of my life than I would consider sticking my hand in a buzz saw — it would hurt (me) too much. Oneness is a goal of marriage but too often, it is confused with happiness. Sometimes, couples strive for personal happiness at the expense of unity. If they make oneness their priority, happiness will come as a by-product, a serendipity.

### 3. A wife is SUBMISSIVE to her husband.

A wife is in submission to her husband because she was made *from* man. Paul refers to this when he says, "For man did not come from woman, but woman from man; neither was man created for woman, but woman for man" (1 Cor. 11:8, 9, NIV). The scriptures are plain:

Wives, be subject to your husbands, as to the Lord. For the husband is the head of the wife as Christ is the head of the church, his body, and is himself its Savior. As the church is subject to Christ, so let wives also be subject in everything to their husbands.

Ephesians 5:22-24

C.S. Lewis gives us a beautiful view of biblical authority in the marriage relationship.

The two sexes meet in the marriage union. There the masculine is given authority over the feminine as Christ has authority over the church. The male is responsible to love his wife and give himself for her as Christ gave himself for the church. It is because of this sacrifice that the husband may ask obedience of his wife. The obedience is the humility of the wife and must be matched by the humility of the husband, her lover. The obedience is not a subsuming of the wife's personality by her husband but a union of both personalities into a new one. . . .

In the marriage union the authority is held by the man, but servitude belongs to both. As Christ served the church, so the man must serve the woman as she serves him . . . Both must have humility . . . Yet when a decision must be made between the roles, the authority of the man dominates because the characteristics of the sexes demand it.[1]

Women sometimes feel this teaching is unfair. And they rebel, not because of the scripture, but because their husbands abuse it. Some husbands *assume* these scriptures make them Lord God of their wives. Most husbands are not aware that the Bible also teaches *mutual* subjection. There may be times when husbands need to be in subjection to their wives (1 Cor. 7:3). In fact, Paul says in Ephesians 5:21, "Honor Christ by *submitting to each other*."

---

### *"Most husbands are not aware that the Bible also teaches mutual subjection."*

---

Suppose you are racing one mile, and your head says to your body, "You can run a four-minute mile." Your body questions this possibility, but tries. Your body gives all it has, the lungs pump, the heart pounds, the legs ache; but your body crosses the finish line after four minutes. Can you imagine the head becoming outraged and demanding the body

43

re-run the race — this time in less than four minutes? Just as there are times when the head must consider the needs of the body, in the same way, the husband must consider the needs of his wife.

Submission does not mean inferiority. Christ was in subjection to his Father. But Jesus was not inferior to God — indeed he was God (John 1:1-4). I am in subjection to the head of a department at the university where I teach, but that does not mean I am inferior to him. In fact, I can do things he cannot do, and he can do things I cannot do. But when a decision needs to be made regarding important departmental matters, he has the final authority; and I am glad.

---

**"Subjection does not mean inferiority. . . .**
**Jesus was not inferior to God . . . ."**

---

### 4. A wife is a JOINT HEIR with Christ (Rom. 8:17).

Wives are worth just as much to God as husbands. "There is neither male nor female, for you are all one in Christ Jesus" (Gal. 3:28). In heaven there is no giving in marriage; all rejoice in the equal relationship to each other and God (Matt. 22:30). Even on earth, the husband is not a lord but a leader. He should lead like Jesus did — from the position of a servant.

> Now that I, your Lord and Teacher, have washed your feet, you also should wash one another's feet. I have set you an example that you should do as I have done for you. I tell you the truth, no servant is greater than his master, nor is a messenger greater than the one

who sent him. Now that you know these things, you will be blessed if you do them.

John 13:14-17, NIV

When a man forces his wife to do his will, he denies her the responsibility of making her own choices. Adam was wrong to blame Eve because he ate the fruit (Gen. 3:12), and Ammon was wrong to force Tamar to commit fornication with him (2 Sam 13:10-15). God gave woman the privilege of making important decisions. Abigail was married to a foolish husband, but she loved and defended him. However, his rejections of her judgment cost him his wealth and his life. Had he listened to Abigail, he would have been richly blessed (1 Sam. 25). Countless men think submission means that women are inferior in reason or judgment — a serious misunderstanding that has caused much needless resentment in wives. Wives are a gift from God. To fail to listen to them and to fail to allow them to use their God-given talents is to misuse the gift and frustrate both the wife and God.

> The husband should be a dominant figure in the life of his family, even though he should not be dominating. He should be a leader without being a dictator. He should be the head of the home, while carefully preserving the equal rights and privileges of his wife. He should be the decision-maker, after careful and thorough consultation and agreement with his partner. Without these basic characteristics, it is extremely doubtful whether any man can fulfill the role of husband.[2]

### 5. A wife is her husband's HELPER.

God said he would make a companion for man, a "helper fit for him" (Gen. 2:18). This role indicates that the woman assumes a responsible position by the man's side — not under his foot. God says the woman is to fill the man's *needs*, not his *wants*. What a man wants may not be what he needs. A husband must accept the help of his wife, even though she is not perfect. It might even be through her mistakes and weaknesses that the husband learns how to forgive and to be gracious.

**6. A wife is CHOSEN by her husband.**

As God has carefully chosen his people through faith (2 Thess. 2:13), so a husband carefully chooses his wife. She will wear his name, bear his children, and give power to his influence and heart to his countenance. Any person will not do. Dating and engagement are important times because he must weigh all the data, using his head and his heart to choose this special person who will have a tremendous influence on the direction of his life. The choice is made for life, "until death do us part."

---

*"To blame her for not living up to his expectations is a reflection more on his choice than her behavior."*

---

After the choice and the vows, the husband *still chooses her!* His *continual* choosing of her changes her — like a rosebud opening into full bloom. Should he change his choice to another woman or try to make his wife into something other than what he chose, he destroys her and their relationship.

To blame her for not living up to *his* expectations is a reflection more on his choice than her behavior. Any choice is limiting. To choose *this* is not to choose *that*. The place to "unchoose" is *before* the vows. Unless you are willing to honor the choice — don't choose.

46

In a worldly marriage, a man can choose to give his love to a woman for a night, a month, or until his good feelings wear off. But Christians choose to give their love for life, the only choice that brings love to maturity. To choose *conditionally* (as in worldly marriages) creates uncertainty; the spouse never knows when the choice will end. The wife lives nervously on the edge of not knowing, creating emotional exhaustion. The marriage is threatened before it begins.

### 7. A wife is COMMITTED to her husband.

The wife has a choice in selecting whom she will give her love to. Once selected, she enters into a covenant with God to love her husband until death. This seems hard only to those who do not understand the nature of love. Love can be pledged or vowed. Love is not a feeling that comes and goes. Marital love is *active good will* toward the other. Love is finding out what the other needs — and supplying it. We love our children unconditionally, despite their actions. God loved us unconditionally, despite our sins. We show love for our spouse by overlooking and/or forgiving his or her faults, which becomes a bonding agent that makes us one. This commitment to love cannot be demanded — it must be given.

When a wife pledges to love her husband till death, it does not mean that she must be perfect in her love. The covenant of love gives her hope and promise that when she fails it would not be a cause for separation or divorce. In the same way, when the husband pledges his love to his wife, the covenant extends the same promise.

The Bible says that the husband is to leave his father and mother and *"cleave"* to his wife (Gen. 2:24). No marriage experiment has any validity if it lacks the essential ingredient of total and irrevocable commitment. Karl Barth defines marriage as:

> The form of encounter of male and female in which the free, mutual, harmonious choice of love on the part of a particular man and woman leads to a responsibly undertaken life-union which is lasting, complete, and exclusive. It is the telos, the goal and center of the relationship between man and woman.[3]

### 8. A wife is a SINNER.

A woman is a sinner just as the man is. There's nobody else to marry. Things went wrong back in the garden, and all of us have been warped by sin ever since. The wife will be no more perfect than the husband: "since all have sinned and fall short. . ." (Rom. 3:23).

No doubt, on occasions husbands have made a mental list of all the shortcomings of their wives. Such-a list might include: talks too much, late for appointments, asks dumb questions, embarrasses me, broods too much, cries too easily (ad infinitum). To make a mental list is bad enough; to recite them to her when things go bad is even worse.

---

### *"To not accept the wife's weaknesses is not to accept her at all."*

---

Love that has known no sorrow has no depth. Even sin has its good points — after it has been overcome. It teaches humility, patience, long suffering, forgiveness, acceptance, and love. To not accept the wife's weaknesses is not to accept her at all. One must love the whole package — warts and all — or it's not marital love. When a child is born, godly parents love the child because it is theirs, not because it is beautiful or intelligent. The child might

48

develop some terrible disease, but still the parents love the child. That is the nature of mature love. God's love never departs because one is overweight, uncultured, or a sinner.

The Pharisees, and even Jesus' disciples, had a hard time understanding this concept. They couldn't understand Jesus' association with the sinful woman at Simon's house (Luke 7:36ff.), the woman with five husbands (John 4:7ff.), or the woman taken in the act of adultery (John 8:3ff.). A good husband must learn to love his wife because she is *his*, and his love will *make* of her what God wants her to be. When a husband accepts his wife *with her weaknesses,* it releases him from reacting negatively to her weaknesses and releases his wife from the desperation of trying to live up to *his* standards instead of *God's.*

### 9. A wife is an INDIVIDUAL.

When a woman becomes a wife, she does not lose her individual personality. The man and woman become one, but both maintain individual personhood. Differences of views and feelings are not bad. After all, that is what gives us something to discuss, review, change, and grow toward. Who would enjoy being married to the "spittin' image" of himself? It is not a compliment to take on the image of another to avoid hassels. This is to become a non-person — to be subsumed, even if it is done voluntarily.

### 10. A wife is PLEDGED TO GOD.

The greatest compliment a wife can give to her husband is not the pledge to love him till "death do us part." It is to "love God till I die." The husband must be placed in the proper perspective. He is not a savior; *God* is savior of her life. God, not the husband, gives ultimate meaning, purpose, and personhood.

She who serves God first serves her husband best.

In her excellent book, *Let Me Be A Woman*, Elizabeth Elliot mentions Betty Scott Stam's prayer, which illustrates the ideal wife's devotion to her God.

> Lord, I give up all my own plans and purposes, all my own desires and hopes, and accept Thy will for my life. I give myself, my life, my all utterly to Thee to be Thine forever. Fill me and seal me with Thy Holy Spirit. Use me as Thou wilt, send me where Thou wilt, work out Thy whole will in my life at any cost, now and forever.[4]

## 11. A wife is a WOMAN.

Is it just an accident that men marry women instead of men? Even in secular society, it is considered abnormal for men to marry men. There are many biological differences between men and women. Generally, women have a smaller stature, a smaller set of lungs, and a different skeletal structure (shorter head, broader face, chin less protruding). A woman has a larger stomach, kidneys, liver, and appendix. Her heart beats more rapidly. As James Dobson said, "Males and females differ biochemically, anatomically, and emotionally. In truth, they are unique in every cell of their bodies, for men carry a different chromosomal pattern than women."[5]

Because men marry women, they cannot effectively treat women like men. An incident that would make a man "stompin' mad" might make a woman depressed. What would make him shout with joy would cause her to weep. A woman uses her "feelings" or "intuition" to make a decision. It doesn't make "sense" that her intuition could win out over reason. When it does, men exclaim, "I don't understand women." Right again! They are not expected to fully understand them — just love them. This mystery is part of the lovable, the different, and the exciting aspect of women. Thank God men marry women.

## 12. A wife is a LOVER.

(The girl:) O that you would kiss me with the kisses of your mouth! For your love is better than wine, your anointing oils are fragrant, your name is oil poured out; therefore the maidens love you. Draw me after you, let us make haste. . . .

The Song of Solomon 1:2-4

Let your fountain be blessed, and rejoice in the wife of your youth, a lovely hind, a graceful doe. Let her affection fill you at all times with delight, be infatuated always with her love.

Proverbs 5:18-19

My beloved put his hand to the latch, and my heart was thrilled within me.

The Song of Solomon 5:4

Another difference between husbands and wives is the way each looks at love — or what each considers a "lover" to be. Husbands associate erotic love with such words as viril, gusto, gallant, and sometimes brash and quick. This concept of erotic love is not ungodly unless it becomes selfish. Wives, on the other hand, associate erotic love with such words as charm, beauty, desire, enchantment, and romance. They use terms that are more fragile, mysterious, vague and more difficult to understand. The husband tends to look mechanically and reasonably at lovemaking; the wife looks more deeply, "spiritually."

51

For a man to get to know his wife as a lover, he must enter her world of love — look through her eyes, feel her romantic love. Otherwise, he is on the outside looking in — never understanding, always missing out. Husbands are sometimes tuned in to an A.M. "hard rock" station, while their wives are listening to F.M. mood music. Lovers need to learn to enjoy each other's music.

**13. A wife is a CONFIDANT.**

One of my greatest comforts is that I have a confidant in my wife. When I was in trouble "up to my neck" in a little church where I was preaching, I could share with no one without hurting someone's feelings, but I could tell her with no fear of being criticized and with no fear that anything I shared would go beyond her lips. A confidant like that is priceless. Where would one "buy" such? No marriage counselor, psychiatrist, or psychologist could earn such confidence. A possession like that is priceless — she is a wife.

When I have silly little hunches, ideas, or feelings about myself, others, and even God, I share with my wife, who will not laugh. Everyone needs a "bounce board" to try out ideas or feelings — a bounce board that is understanding, doesn't laugh at your mistakes nor tells the "hilarious" to friends as the butt of a joke. Safe, secure, warm, and trustworthy are words that describe the feeling when you have a confidant. Such a confidant is found in a man's wife.

**14. A wife is A CHILD BEARER.**

A woman bears children in her husband's name. She provides the "nest" for the little one. She eats the right food, watches her weight, and gets the right exercise as she prepares for the big event. And after the child is born, she assumes major responsibility for care and feeding.

What a debt a proud father owes to his wife as *she* walks through the "valley of death" to deliver the son that will keep his family name alive.

The wife is also the primary child rearer. Most fathers are away earning a living while most wives are at home loving and caring for the children. A wife best provides for the deep emotional needs of the young child. She is unique and that uniqueness is found only in a wife.

---

[1]Joan Lloyd, "Transcendent Sexuality as C.S. Lewis Saw It," *Christianity Today* (November 9, 1973).

[2]Alexander A. Schneiders, "Roles and Role Relationships in Marriage," in *Marital Counseling: Psychology, Ideology, Science* (Springfield: Thomas, 1967), p. 88.

[3]Elizabeth Elliot, *Let Me Be a Woman* (Wheaton: Tyndale, 1976), p. 76.

[4]Elliot, p. 10.

[5]James Dobson, *What Wives Wish Their Husbands Knew About Women* (Wheaton: Tyndale, 1975), pp. 132-133.

# I Am Somebody
## —Self-esteem

### Chapter 4

What a person thinks of himself is important. The Bible says, "For as he thinketh in his heart, so is he" (Prov. 23:7, KJV). We live our lives according to the mental picture we have of ourselves, so it is important to see ourselves as we really are — no misrepresentation. We are not to think more *highly* of ourselves than we ought (Rom. 12:3). But as "children of God," we are also not to think more *lowly* of ourselves than we ought. Dorothy Briggs says, "High self-esteem is not a noisy conceit. It is a quiet sense of self-respect, a feeling of self-worth. When you have it deep inside, you're glad you are you."

Maxwell Maltz, author of *Psycho-Cybernetics*, wrote, "Self-image is the key to human personality and human behavior. Change the self-image and you change the personality and the behavior." He continues saying:

> But more than this, the "self-image" sets the boundaries of individual accomplishment. It

defines what you can and cannot do. Expand the self-image and you expand the area of the possible. The development of an adequate, realistic self-image will seem to imbue the individual with new capabilities and new talents and literally turn failure into success.[1]

People with high self-esteem tend to have fewer illnesses. They are happier, are more successful, have a better family life, and make better decisions than those with low self-esteem.

People with low self-esteem have a hard time accepting compliments. They tend to make excuses for why they look nice, want their opinions verified by others, and refrain from buying something nice for themselves because they do not feel worthy. A person of low self-esteem accepts unworthy labels for himself, such as "Dummie," "Chubbie," "Skinny," "Silly."

People with exaggerated self-esteem or pride are characterized by a haughty spirit, an exaggerated compulsion to achieve, an overinflated ego, vainness, haughtiness; and they ultimately lose what they really want — self-esteem. Often these people are hiding a low self-esteem behind the mask of the "know it all." Once a young student came to me with symptoms of depression. He said things had been going well in the dormitory until "just lately" when his friends began calling him "God." He realized that something was "dreadfully wrong." After talking with some of the boys, he learned that they could no longer tolerate a "guy who had answers to all questions." They decided that if he had all the answers he must be God, so they started "addressing him by his proper name." It was crushing to the young student. He really had a low opinion of himself, and he was causing his own downfall by overcompensating for his low self-esteem.

Another form of improper self-esteem is "pseudo-low self-esteem." Instead of acting better than another, a person with pseudo-low self-esteem acts worse than another. He uses self-effacement to get attention. Usually, the person who depreciates himself only appears to feel inferior. He is consciously or unconsciously reaching for a sympathetic response. When someone says, "I'm so useless, no one really cares what happens to me," he is really craving for someone to answer, "I care for you."

In response to a compliment, the person with pseudo-low self-esteem will respond, "Oh, you are just being nice," or "You don't really understand." These are invitations for more compliments: "I'm not just being nice; I really meant that."

The person practicing self-effacement also does it by being silent, pouting, or standing at a distance from others. These kinds of behavior call attention to him. He extends an invitation to some good-hearted soul to respond with sympathy. He also gets his feelings hurt easily, which is another attention-getting device. It puts pressure on others to apologize and make up to him. He holds grudges; and this gives him an opportunity to get attention from all who will listen to him about how badly he has been treated by the government, his wife, his employer, and his doctor. Creath Davis said:

> Much of our energy is spent trying to convince ourselves and others that we are significant because deep down we fear that we are not. This keeps our attention upon ourselves, which is destructive. If we had proper love of self, then we could focus our attention upon those around us, and seek to understand them and to meet their needs. This is the secret of truly great men. The man who knows he is important need not work at proving his importance.

He can serve others, irrespective of whether they recognize his worth or not. Every man is important, but no man is all-important. The real thing is to be a person of worth in Christ, not simply to give that impression.[2]

The person who loves himself, biblically, is able to effectively love others. We see a perfect example of this in Christ.

## The Ideal Self-Esteem

Three, interlocking circles would illustrate the ideal of self-esteem. Security, significance, and competence suggest three items that all of us strive for. A healthy portion of each of these is needed for good self-esteem.

### Security

Therefore, since we are justified by faith, *we have peace* with God through our Lord Jesus Christ. Through whom we have obtained access *to this grace* in which we stand . . . .

Romans 5:1,2

There is therefore now *no condemnation* for those who are in Christ Jesus, . . . .

Romans 8:1

Who shall separate us from the love of Christ? . . . we are more than conquerors through him who loved us. For I am sure that neither death, nor life, nor angels, nor principalities, nor things present, nor things to come, nor powers, nor height, nor depth, *nor anything else in all creation, will be able to separate us from the love of God* in Christ Jesus our Lord.

Romans 8:35-39

## Significance

... You are a *chosen race*, a *royal priesthood*, a *holy nation*, God's own people, that you may declare the wonderful deeds of him who called you out of darkness into his wonderful light. Once you were no people but now *you are God's people*; once you had not received mercy but now you have received mercy.

1 Peter 2:9,10

For all who are led by the Spirit of God are *sons of God*. For you did not receive the spirit of slavery to fall back into fear, but you have received the spirit of sonship ... the Spirit himself bearing witness with our spirit that we are children of God, and if children, then heirs, heirs of God and fellow heirs with Christ . . . .

Romans 8:14-17

## Competence

I *can do all things* in him who strengthens me.

Philippians 4:13

And my God will supply every need of yours according to his riches in glory in Christ Jesus.

Philippians 4:19

For God did not give us a spirit of timidity but a spirit of power and love and self-control.

2 Timothy 1:7

# The Child and Self-Esteem

When I was a child, I thought my mouth was too big for my face. No one else had such a big mouth, I thought, so I must be an "odd ball." I'll never forget the day "Miss Auntie," my first-grade teacher, shouted at Ruth, one of my classmates, for wetting her pants. I nearly died! I knew I'd be the point of her wrath someday! Then, when I was in the third grade, I became ill and missed six weeks of school. When I returned, I didn't do well. My classmates "graduated" to the fourth grade, but I didn't. I had to repeat the third grade. Thus, I was separated from Paul, my best friend, which was another blow to my already diminishing ego.

As we grow up, we store mental tape recordings of data we consider important about ourselves and replay these tapes over and over as the years go by. More importantly, *we live our lives according to these tapes.* This presents some real problems. These tapes are not the real "me" because:

**1. We allow the thoughts of outside sources to take precedence over our own thoughts.** Our self-image does not judge the source and does not decide what to record and what not to record. Like a computer, it just accepts the false data as truth.

**2. We choose to tape more negative thoughts about ourselves than positive.** When asked to make a list of their positive and negative qualities, most people have a longer list of negatives than positives. Try it and see. It is a good way to begin studying **your** self-image.

**3. We permit negative comments to carry more weight than positive comments.** Which do you remember more readily, a pointed criticism or a nice compliment? I have asked hundreds of people this questions, and it is apparent that criticism makes a stronger impression. Criticism carries more impression power — they are taped with louder volume. We may have received far more compliments than criticisms, but we don't remember them as well because they are overcome by the power of criticism.

**4. We rationalize our compliments.** For some strange reason, we turn down the volume when recording compliments. We think to ourselves: "If

they really knew me, they wouldn't say that.";
"They are just being kind to me."; "They are just
trying to butter me up." We do not accept compliments with the same intensity or validity that we
accept criticisms.

5. **We misunderstand the statements of others
easily.** When a person starts down the road toward a
poor self-image, he tends to give neutral data a negative tint. He is suspicious of a casual statement or
jest. People with low self-esteem tend to develop
what might be called a mild paranoia. If there is a
question about what others have said about them,
they interpret it as criticism instead of as a compliment.

## Improving Self-Esteem

Here are some ways parents can help children
"record better tapes."

**Provide a secure environment.** This means hugging, patting, and loving. Infants should be breastfed if possible. The old-fashioned rocking chair has
helped millions of children to be nourished with security.

**Try to understand them.** Develop the ability to
"get behind their eyeballs" — to see through their
eyes, to hear with their ears, and to hurt from their
nerve endings. Try to sense their feelings so that
your child will never say, "but Dad, you don't understand."

**Be patient.** Patience allows us to endure troubles
without coming unglued, even in prolonged troubles.
It refuses to allow us to blow up, become rude, or be
harsh.

**Have faith in them.** Ultimately, faith comes from
God; but it must be transferred to our children. We
believe in them, even when there is little or no reason to substantiate it, because faith creates more

faith. To continually question and doubt our children will create self-doubt in them. Christ believed in Peter and named him "rock" when he was still a sandpile.

**Be open and transparent.** When you are truthful with your words and feelings, you create an honest atmosphere, which assures security. You create suspicion when you hold back and reserve your feelings. Psychologists say we reveal ourselves in our feelings more than with our words.

**Praise and compliment them.** Look for honest opportunities to praise your child. The harder you look, the more you will find. Try your best to keep criticism to a minimum, even when deserved. All of us function more efficiently in an atmosphere of acceptance. Criticism is like poison, a little goes a long way. Praise seems to come out in the wash, while criticism sticks in our memory like indelible ink.

**Avoid labeling.** When we lose patience with a child, we often attach labels, such as "How could you be so dumb?" or "How stupid can you get?" One university co-ed labeled herself as "big, fat, and ugly." She was none of these, but she got that image of herself from her parents! Most of us label ourselves bad enough without parents making it worse. If we must label a child, label positively. "You are a knockout today, sweetheart." Also, remember to make your label believable, or it will create suspicion.

For more information about how to help your child's self-esteem, read *Hide or Seek* by James Dobson or *Your Child's Self-Esteem* by Dorothy Briggs.

Retired people and the aged, the second most neglected group in our society, also need to know that they are secure, significant, and competent. Hopefully, the suggestions in this chapter for helping children can be modified to help the old develop a good self-esteem.

## Barriers To Self-Esteem

**Irrational Goals.** We need to plan ahead and strive for goals that are beyond us, but it's foolish to set impossible goals. Some of us set audacious goals. When an individual thinks that everyone must like him, he has set such a goal. It is easier to be president of the U.S.A. than to be liked by everyone. Our self-esteem must not be tied to unreasonable goals.

Jesus lived a perfect life, but many people were enraged by him and eventually crucified him. If people were angered at the perfect model, there will be many others displeased with his imperfect disciples.

Some parents set impossible goals, thinking that their children must be perfect. If their children embarrass them, even during the difficult adolescent years, they assume total responsibility for the failures. This is unreasonable. Self-esteem must not be determined by the success or failure of our children. God recognized that David's children might turn out badly, but this did not hinder God's love and appreciation for David (Ps. 89). Too often, Proverb 22:6 ("Train up a child in the way he should go, and when he is old he will not depart from it.") is quoted to inflict undue guilt on parents. What parents need is help with their wayward children, not more criticism and guilt.

Parents are only partially responsible for the way children turn out. Neighbors, teachers, friends, the media, the devil, and a child's own self-will help determine the eventual outcome of our children. A Christian parent should not assume undue guilt for children who turn out badly anymore than they should take full credit when they turn out right.

Many times *our* goals and needs are never met; but *God's goal* for us can be met. When our goals become God's goals, they are guaranteed attainable. When our goal is to live under the lordship of Jesus, our children will probably turn out right — but even that alone should not determine our self-esteem.

**External Circumstances Beyond My Control.** A flood destroys valuable property and precious lives. A young hoodlum grabs a gun away from an old night watchman and kills him. Why would God allow things like this to happen to Christian people? When we are psychologically insulted, we strike back with anger or languish in depression. But we must not take these external circumstances personally.

---

### *"It is not what happens to a Christian that counts but his attitude toward what happens."*

---

In a lumberyard one day, I heard two men talking. One asked, "Have you been to church lately?" The other responded, "No, not since my father died. God knew how much I loved my father. I haven't been back to church since." This man had taken the death of his father as an indication that God didn't love him anymore. From the tone of his voice it seemed that the man was trying to punish God by not going to church anymore. Just as God allows good things to happen to sinners (Matt. 5:45), he allows bad things to happen to Christians. It is not what happens to a Christian that counts but his *attitude* toward what happens. When God allowed Satan to strip Job of everything — his lands, cattle, children, and even his health — Job didn't pout. His response was not self-condemnation but glorification of God: " . . . the Lord gave, and the Lord has taken away; blessed be the name of the Lord" (Job 1:21).

**Cultural Assumptions.** Our American culture includes many forces that cause us to yearn for things we don't really need. Four of them are: money or riches, beauty, intelligence, and athletic ability. These are main items in our daily diet of newspapers, magazines, and tv. Despite the fact that beautiful, rich, and intelligent people often suffer from depression, low self-esteem, and even suicide, Madison Avenue still sells this lie to most Americans. If it is true that "things" bring us happiness, then the masses of the world are doomed to misery. Thankfully, Jesus came to the world to share "life abundantly" with *all* people — rich or poor, literate or illiterate, pretty or ugly.

Those who were culturally gifted, the "wise and mighty" of the world, rejected the message of Jesus (1 Cor. 1:26-31). Simple people, who were not cumbered with possessions and worldly aspirations, "heard him gladly." The Bible seems to imply that common people have the best chance of attaining a healthy self-esteem. The rich young ruler's possessions stood in his way to happiness (Luke 18:18-30). The poor, sick, afflicted, maimed, lame, and blind went away healed and rejoicing. It's just easier for a poor man to be humble (James 2:5-7; 1 Tim. 6:17-19).

Satan tricks Christian people into thinking that they can have the best of both worlds. He wants us to believe that we can attain worldly success and godly recognition at the same time. I believe Satan allows a few men to "hit the jackpot" so that the rest of us will gamble that we, too, can attain success in both worlds. But Jesus says, ". . . You cannot serve God and mammon" (Matt. 6:24).

Accepting the American concept of success causes several problems. First, cultural assumptions are fickle. They change from one year to the next. The "in" thing this year is the "out" thing next year. It is impossible to build a stable personality on a fluctuating assumption.

Secondly, cultural assumptions are short-term for they age and die within a life span. All mankind is in a trajectory of death. Faith is the only thing that provides a resolution to the problem of death.

Thirdly, earthly assumptions are a lie. Significance, security, and competence do *not* come by attaining wealth, intelligence, beauty, or ability. These things alone are not bad but neither are they good. They are neutral. It is our attitude toward them and how we use them that determine their worth. Our cultural assumptions mask the real problem of sin. It is like putting cosmetics on cancer, which does not cure. The cosmetic is neutral; yet when it is used to disguise cancer, it perpetrates a lie. It suggests health when there is none. So wealth, beauty, intelligence, wit, and athletic ability only give the impression of success. The truth is that "every good endowment and every perfect gift is from above . . . " (James 1:17).

**Neurotic Guilt.** Psychiatrist Karl Menninger recognizes the reality of sin. He believes that guilt is a natural and good consequence for transgression of moral and ethical codes of conduct.[3]

But there is another type of guilt called neurotic or false guilt, which is not good because it destroys our self-esteem. It is a feeling of guilt when actually there is no guilt. When I was a child, my mother allowed me to walk several blocks to my father's grocery store to buy each of us a treat. She wanted a Coke, and I chose an ice-cream bar. Being excited and proud, I wasn't going to eat my ice cream until I got home so we could enjoy our treats together. As I hurried along, the Coke bottle slipped from my hands and broke on the walk a few houses from home. I was crushed and felt guilty. In tears, I offered my mother the ice-cream bar, but I knew she wanted the Coke — there was no redemption. I can still feel the hurt and disappointment. But that incident was not real guilt — despite my feelings. Things like that happen to all of us. We become disappointed, hurt, and crushed over many similar incidents; but we must not attach *sin* and guilt to them.

The Bible says we should not lust. But some people think that even if they *look*, it is a sin of lust. The Bible also says we should not hate, and some Christians feel guilty when they get angry. People with a low self-image accuse themselves when *anything* goes wrong. This is irrational and an unbiblical way of thinking. *Feeling* guilty does not determine guilt anymore than "feeling saved" determines salvation. There must be an actual transgression against God or your fellow man before you can assume real guilt. To assume guilt just because you feel bad about yourself is a miserable way to live. It is usually harder for us to forgive ourselves than to forgive others. Ardis Whitman wrote:

> We excuse a multitude of sins in others and keep our greatest anger for ourselves. We brood over what we've done and what we've left undone; over the hurts we've brought to others and the damage we've brought to ourselves; over the steady drip, drip of our inadequacy and over the inability to get rid of whatever faults we may have.

**Self-Judgment.** God doesn't want you to judge yourself. He is the specialist in judging people's worth. Most of us judge ourselves too harshly, like the man in the parable of the pounds. Jesus tells about a nobleman who gave ten of his servants a pound each and said to them, "Trade with these till I come."

When the nobleman returned, "The first came before him, saying, 'Lord, your pound has made ten pounds more.' . . . And the second came, saying, 'Lord, your pound has made five pounds.' . . . Then another came, saying, 'Lord, here is your pound, which I kept laid away in a napkin; for I was afraid of you, because you are a severe man; you take up what you did not lay down, and reap what you did not sow' " (Luke 19:11-25).

The nobleman in this parable represents God, and God did not ask the man to do anything he was incapable of doing. The man *judged himself incapable*! His low self-esteem cost him not only his reward but gave him an excuse to lay false charges against God.

In Luke 15, Jesus tells another story of self-judgment. A young son requested his inheritance and then wasted it in riotous living. His evaluation of himself appeared to be high. But, as is often the case, deep within, the young prodigal felt inadequate and went on a splurge to prove he was capable of running his own affairs. Eventually, he was proven wrong and his self-image grew worse. He found himself with no friends but the hogs. Then, he "came to himself" and realized who he was—the son of a nobleman. For the first time in his life he was humble (" . . . I have sinned . . . I am no longer worthy to be called your son.") and accepted *his father's evaluation* (vss. 22-24).

God's evaluation, not ours, is the key. God has judged us worthy to carry the gospel to the world, even though we are not perfect. Not even to angels did he give this glorious task. He calls us his sons, his heirs, even co-heirs with Christ (Rom. 8:14-17). The apostles lacked faith, fled in the face of troubles, denied the Lord, cussed and swore, but Jesus never took away their self-esteem. He pronounced them capable.

Paul speaks of Christ's disciples as "afflicted in every way, but not crushed; perplexed, but not driven to despair; persecuted, but not forsaken; struck down, but not destroyed" (2 Cor. 4:8,9). While Christ desires humility, he never wants us crushed or driven to despair. Christ preserves our personal worth and dignity. To a great extent, what we think of ourselves determines our ability to fulfill the task Christ wants us to complete. God, like the father in the parable of the prodigal son, sees something in us we cannot see; and his love is going to bring it forth.

---

*"Our eternal destiny is not determined by our performance in the past, present, or future but by how . . . we respond to how much he loves and values us."*

---

We can never be worthy of his love, and God's love of the unworthy is the prime motivation for Christianity. If we have to be worthy of God's love there can be neither self-esteem, nor hope. If we could become twice as good tomorrow as we are today and twice as good each succeeding day for the next thirty years, God would not love us anymore than he does today. God loved David just as much when he was an adulterer as when he was a prophet, king, and poet. Our eternal destiny is not determined by our performance in the past, present, or future, but by how gratefully we respond to how much he loves and values us. It is important to add, however, that the more like Jesus we become, the more we will like ourselves and the more others will like us. It then follows that when we like ourselves, we will become more effective in influencing others to be like Jesus.

God's message to people of low self-esteem is to stop being our own judge and jury. He wants us to stop handcuffing ourselves with inferiority feelings. God has judged us worthy to die for. "We love, (not because we are worthy but) because he first loved us" (1 John 4:19).

## Self-Esteem and the Community of Believers

If success and self-esteem are not found by worldly methods, then how can they be found? The Christian believes that God provided the church as a collection of people with faith in God to help each other maintain a good mental picture of themselves. The Christian community is a therapeutic community, a place of health and encouragement. It is a place where "good news" (not bad) is preached.

It is almost impossible to have honest self-esteem unless we can receive love from others and give love to others. Bruce Narramore said:

> I am convinced that one reason God instructs us to love each other is to communicate a sense of value to each other. God's very nature is to love. He created us, he loves us, he values us, and he expects us to return that love to each other.

Jesus said, "This is my commandment, that you love one another as I have loved you. Greater love has no man than this, that a man lay down his life for his friends" (John 15:12-13).

It takes people who care, not things, to cure emotional and spiritual problems (Gal. 6:1-3). God wants members of his family to minister to and love one another. He designed the church to be a place where people refuse to lord it over one another (1 Pet. 5:3,5).

Millions of people, who are lonely and heartbroken today, could be healed if they would allow God's people to love them. As we learn to love ourselves, we must allow others to demonstrate their love toward us. Just because we have been hurt by someone doesn't mean that everyone will hurt us. Someone once said, "As by others we are broken, so by others are we healed." If you have difficulty acquiring self-esteem, try sharing yourself lovingly and completely with a few trusted friends in the community of Christ.

## Some Practical Helps

Here are some practical suggestions that might help you win your struggle with low self-esteem.

1. **Be careful how you think.** Think positive. "For as (a man) thinketh in his heart, so is he . . ." (Prov. 23:7). Cast your mind in God's direction; your belief system and feelings will follow.

2. **Believe that your self-esteem can be changed.** "I can do all things in him who strengthens me" (Phil. 4:13).

3. **Start moving.** Do things that will make you like yourself. We can begin to "love (our) enemies, and do good, and lend, expecting nothing in return . . ." (Luke 6:35). The reward will be worth it.

4. **Risk yourself.** Peter would never have walked on the water if he had not risked himself. Even when he failed, it was worth it. Who else besides Christ can claim to have walked on water? Some of the greatest lessons ever learned came through failure. Great faith demands great risks. Risk being embarrassed or saying "no" when you need to; risk taking a stand for Christ when you are in enemy territory.

5. **Stop being critical.** Paul pleads with the Romans to "stop passing judgment on one another" (Rom. 14:13, NIV).

6. **Start noticing others.** People with bad self-images dwell on their own negative attributes. Even though they outwardly deny themselves any righteousness, they often are the most selfish of all. Reversing the process will help. Start noticing others,

especially their good qualities. Compliment these good qualities, and you will be amazed at the transformation that takes place in your own life.

7. **Forget mistakes.** All of us make mistakes. Satan likes for us to worry over them because it makes us doubt ourselves. There is a difference between "learning from" and "dwelling on" past mistakes. Paul said, " . . . forgetting what lies behind and straining forward to what lies ahead, I press on toward the goal for the prize . . . " (Phil. 3:13,14).

8. **Know that you don't have to live up to the expectations of others.** You do not have to have an immaculate house like Mrs. Clean. Your children don't have to make straight "A's" like Mr. and Mrs. Einstein's children, nor do they have to be as well disciplined as James Dobson's. You don't have to use time as efficiently as Mr. Computer, nor do you have to serve dinners like Betty Crocker. Our gifts are uniquely ours. We are running a race that all can win. We are not competing against others for our salvation. Christ would have died for you if no one else existed. He only wants you to be the best "you" you can be.

9. **Start going to worship.** God provides people to help you, so don't neglect this help.

10. **Realize that life is not always fair.** God allows unexplanable things to happen to both good and evil people. What counts is not what happens, but our attitude toward what happens.

11. **Put an end to procrastination.** Waiting "till the rains come" to plant the seed will result in crop failure. Plant many good deeds; and in time, they will bear fruit. Begin now!

---

[1]Maxwell Maltz, *Psycho-Cybernetics* (New York: Essandess), p. 11.

[2]Creath Davis, *Beyond This God Cannot Go* (Kentwood: Zondervan, 1973), p. 65.

[3]Karl Menninger, *Whatever Became of Sin* (New York: Hawthorn, 1973).

[4]Ardis Whitman, "The One Person No Woman Forgives," *Woman's Day* (April 24, 1978).

# I Love You
## – Unconditional Love

### Chapter 5

What a flood of emotions break loose when somebody tells me, "I love you." Those three words hold out the promise of the deepest relationship one person can hope to share with another. A profound and beautiful blend of closeness and understanding, warmth and acceptance, pleasure and security — all reaching out to us in a simple affirmation of love.

No wonder, then, that we also feel a sense of risk, of vulnerability, to say or to hear the words "I love you." For we've all experienced love that flourished briefly and then died, love that raised our expectations and called forth commitments, but dissolved and left us hurt and bewildered.

The demands that people place on a word like love almost guarantee that we will sometimes be deceived, betrayed, or let down. If we say we love God, that we love our parents, *and* that we love old movies, hot dogs, and this year's fashions, then we're setting ourselves up for confusion.

In spite of all the pitfalls, the word "love" has special meaning when we refer to human relationships. We were not so old when we first realized our family loved us with a special love. We are shaped for all time by the love we shared with parents, brothers, and sisters as we grew up. Parents take deep satisfaction from being a part of the growth and development of their children.

We also enjoy love for a friend. Most of us remember a special friend who shared many precious experiences with us as we matured. There was the friend we played with before we were old enough to start school. There were the "spend the night" friends from elementary school days and the "can't go anywhere without" friends from junior high school days.

Most of us have a special friend outside our family that we enjoy in a unique way. Sometimes our intimate friends may be far away and hard to reach, but we look forward with great joy to times when we can be together.

We remember "first loves" —those early, hazardous experiences when we thought we might be in love, but were not quite sure how we were supposed to feel or how we were supposed to act. With a little more experience, we became comfortable with the idea of romantic love. Our husband-to-be or wife-to-be came along, and "love for a lifetime" developed into marriage.

## The Source of All Loves

At the heart of all our familiar expressions of love is an uncommon love. It develops in a different way; it unfolds slowly, usually with great difficulty. The way is easier for us if our parents exemplified and helped us to discover for ourselves this special kind of love.

In the Bible, it is called *agape* love. It is spiritual love — love which seeks the highest, greatest good of another person with no strings attached.

In fact, *agape* love is the only kind of love that is totally unconditional. Other forms of love tend to be bound up with conditions: "If you are a good person, I will love you."; "If you give me gifts, I will love you."; "If you live up to my expectations, I will love you."

Conditional love is given in exchange for something the lover wants. The conditions may be slightly different: "I love you because you are so beautiful (or handsome)."; "I love you because you are so talented and successful."; "I love you because you buy me such lovely gifts, take me to such romantic places, treat me like a very important person." Conditional love must be won. And once it is won, conditional love sets up a constant parade of "loveable" acts and attitudes that must continue in order for the love to continue.

But the Bible speaks of an entirely different kind of love. Its source is in God's love for us. God showed his unconditional love for us "while we were yet sinners" (Rom. 5:8). Because agape love comes from God to us, he enables us to show such love to one another. (1 John 4:7,11).

The Bible describes this kind of love in these familiar, yet challenging, words:

Love is patient and kind; love is not jealous or boastful; it is not arrogant or rude. Love does not insist on its own way; it is not irritable or resentful; it does not rejoice at wrong, but rejoices in the right. Love bears all things, believes all things, hopes all things, endures all things.

1 Corinthians 13:4-7

It is interesting to rearrange these "loving" qualities to show what love is and is not, what it does and
doesn't do:

*Love is:*
   Patient
   Kind

*Love does:*
   Rejoice in the right
   Bear all things
   Believe all things
   Hope all things
   Endure all things

*Love is not:*
   Jealous
   Boastful
   Arrogant
   Rude
   Irritable
   Resentful

*Love does not:*
   Insist on its own way
   Rejoice at wrong

## All the Loves In One Relationship

Married love blends all the different kinds of love.
There is a need for sexual attraction between partners. The exhilaration brought by sexuality brings
an important dimension to marriage and God intended for it to be so. Sex is God's idea; he created us
". . . male and female . . ." (Gen. 1:27).

But the Lord realized the danger of either partner
considering the other simply or primarily as a "sex
object." Paul wrote, "That each of you know how to
take a wife in holiness and honor, not in the passion

of lust like heathen who do not know God" (1 Thess. 4:4-5). The sexual relationship has a purpose in marriage, but it is only one focus. Both partners in a marriage are *whole* personalities. In marriage, two people make a commitment to try to discover and meet the widest possible range of needs — sexual, emotional, intellectual, and spiritual.

## Marrying Your Best Friend

Romantic love, so important to the vitality of the marriage relationship, usually matures into friendship. Marriage partners are happiest when they are best friends.

Quite often two people discover (to their horror) that "We just don't love each other any more." In many cases they are saying that their romantic relationship has stagnated, has failed to develop into a deep friendship. Instead, they no longer enjoy going places together and doing things together. Each has been hurt by the other and is afraid of the pain which may be inflicted again at any moment. Often they may retreat into a self-centered routine that creates boredom. Ultimately, they may lose all their common interests or common goals. What could have become a friendship dissolves into a "stalemate."

Every good marriage develops an imaginative variety of ways to keep friendship alive. The more rewarding the friendship, the more time, patience, and perseverance it takes to make it grow. Husbands and wives who enjoy spending time together can learn many ways to be friends. They learn to share their innermost thoughts and dreams without fear of being ridiculed, attacked, or hurt. Someone wrote:

Oh, the comfort, the inexpressible comfort of feeling safe with a person, having neither to weigh thoughts nor measure words, but pouring them all right out, just as they are, chaff and grain together: certain that a faithful hand will take and sift them, keep that which is worth keeping, and then with a breath of kindness, blow the rest away.

When romantic love grows and develops over the years, it is drawing on *agape* love (unconditional love) as a resource. Romantic love, at its best, draws on the permanent commitment two people make to each other. Because they know God's love, each one is not afraid to pledge to act lovingly with the other — regardless of the other's behavior. They trust God to enable them to treat each other with patience, kindness, and unselfishness. They can pledge to love without any strings attached, without waiting for acts that actually deserve a loving response. Romantic love built on that kind of base will continue to grow with every year that passes.

## Green Love Can Ripen

Marriage needs maturity to really prosper. Self-centeredness is a sign of an immature relationship. As two people invest their energies in their relationship, they can overcome the selfishness that threatens so many marriages in the early years.

The divorce rate among people who get married as teenagers is about 85 percent, according to current statistics. It happens to people who need more personal growth before they are ready for marriage. It also happens to people who rush into marriage without allowing time for their relationship to develop before marriage. Tragically, the same immaturity and lack of personal growth that produced a shaky marriage often causes a couple to give up on a marriage before it breaks ground and blossoms.

Immaturity is not an exclusive characteristic of the young. Adults can be immature, too. The husband who still buys things he cannot afford is immature. The whining, complaining wife who constantly picks at her husband is still a child emotionally. And this immaturity will destroy a marriage.

Unconditional love, grounded in the love of God, gives birth to a deep and abiding trust. A marriage relationship cannot flourish without trust.

Trust doesn't come automatically with time. It comes to two people who have had a number of intense experiences together and many opportunities to see each other sacrifice for really important principles. That takes time. And if the two people act in ways that indicate that they cannot trust each other, the relationship may continue, but it cannot be a loving or lasting relationship.

Here are the feelings of people who are looking for trust:

"I feel comfortable with you only when I can trust you with my fears and frustrations, as well as with my hopes, dreams, and longings."

"I am at ease only when I can trust you to accept me when I am not at my best, when there is no fear that you will 'love me less.' "

"When I can be vulnerable with the full assurance that you will not hurt me, I can trust. Only then will I know that our love is not based on superficial things, but on an unconditional commitment. Our relationship can then take on new depth and new dimensions not possible without trust."

## Happiness Is Learned, Not Inherited

A loving, selfless husband or wife should also concentrate on developing his or her disposition. It helps, of course, if you had a happy childhood. Childhood experience helps to develop "the habit of happiness." But anybody can develop the habit of happiness at any time in life. It is a matter of habit. We can take responsibility for our own behavior.

The love of God can motivate us to develop good habits rather than bad ones. Agape love can help us develop a good disposition. It is a matter of the source of power in our lives. Who or what controls us? Are we controlled by our circumstances, by what happens around us? Are we controlled by other people? Are we controlled by some frightening, irresistible power? Or is our trust in God—to remove the barriers from our wills, to set us free, to give us control over our lives? It's "only natural" to take revenge when someone mistreats us. But Jesus showed us how to "love your enemies and pray for those who persecute you" (Matt. 5:44). He's saying, in effect, "you don't have to let what others do control what you do."

---

## *"A bad disposition is a bad habit that has developed from a loveless base."*

---

Peter says, "Do not return evil for evil or reviling for reviling; but on the contrary bless, for to this you have been called" (1 Pet. 3:9).

A bad disposition is a bad habit that has developed from a loveless base. I remember an experience I had one evening in a restaurant. A family — father, mother, two children, and grandmother — came in; and as they entered, it was obvious from the look on the mother's face that she was upset about something. It soon became even more obvious.

The family sat down in a booth. The father stood to take the orders and then went to get their hamburgers and distributed them. When the mother got hers, she immediately unwrapped it and took the top off to see if it was properly prepared. When she discovered that it was not exactly what she wanted,

79

she demanded that her husband return it. With great embarrassment, he exchanged her hamburger and nervously returned it to mother for another inspection. This time it passed inspection. But when the father finally sat down to eat, the mother's anger had spread to him.

This is a typical pattern for immature behavior. The mother's actions may have been a carry-over from some experience earlier in the day — perhaps just before arriving. Most of us identify, at least a little, with her. There have been times when we were bitter because of an unpleasant experience. And we have been ashamed later. But a disposition that cannot recover quickly from frustration mars all our relationships and leaves behind the torn remains of happy occasions that might have been.

## Sharing Pleasure

A husband and wife who are truly friends learn to develop common interests. Sometimes these are interests each person had before they met, but often two people develop interests together. They may start with an interest that one already has, or they may develop an interest agreed upon by both to pursue as an adventure unique to them alone. The more important an interest is to one partner, the more important it is that the other partner find some way to share it.

Shared experiences build relationships. Two people who labor together to achieve a common goal develop a special closeness. Even sharing hardships can build relationships. Many couples recall their survival together during difficult times — military service, schooling, the first job. Sadly, for couples without a sense of common struggle, hard times can create strains and stresses that threaten rather than strengthen.

Obviously, experiences which bring pleasure are

better at building relationships. One evening my wife and I sat watching television, laughing together. We were both in our pajamas — relaxed completely and enjoying the experience. Suddenly, I realized how important it is to have someone to laugh with. It is impossible to really enjoy a good laugh when you are alone. Shared pleasure increases that pleasure and has a positive effect on a relationship.

It is difficult, but not impossible, for someone completely turned-off by opera to spend life happily with a real "opera buff." They might make a good life together by working around this unique problem. It would be better if the opera lover is not forced to give up music.

The same is true of other interests, including religion. If religion is really important to one of the mates, it is vitally important that this religion be shared by the two. Paul says, "Do not be mismated with unbelievers . . ." (2 Cor. 6:14). He talks about the danger of a believer being led astray by the influence of the unbeliever.

But there is another practical matter involved in such a relationship. If the two actively pursue different religions, their most important interests are focused in different directions. What might have been the center of their life together becomes a divisive factor (Matt. 6:33).

## Spiritual Intimacy

Howard and Charlotte Clinebell said, "No single factor does more to give a marriage joy or keep it both a venture and an adventure in mutual fulfillment than shared commitment to spiritual discovery."[1] The joy of going to church together and being involved together in church-related activities brings marriage partners closer. Bible study, prayer, and intimate sharing of the spiritual realities of life allow two people to develop a closeness that is impossible for those who do not share such experiences.

Commitment to a common Lord inevitably brings two people closer to each other. It also draws them to a common center outside themselves, which relieves tremendous pressure in a marriage. By accepting the Bible as a common standard by which to measure the relationship, two people can more easily solve the routine problems of life and open themselves to an intimacy which is otherwise impossible to achieve.

The absence of spiritual commitment produces havoc in an individual's life; and this, in turn, contaminates a person's relationships.

In Romans 1:24-32, the Bible teaches that immorality of all kinds grows out of man's failure to acknowledge God as the Creator and material things as God's creations, which are to be used, not worshiped. People are to be neither used nor worshiped, but respected and loved:

> Therefore God gave them up in the lusts of their hearts to impurity, to the dishonoring of their bodies among themselves, because they exchanged the truth about God for a lie and worshiped and served the creature rather than the Creator, who is blessed for ever! Amen. For this reason God gave them up to dishonorable passions. Their women exchanged natural relations for unnatural, and the men likewise gave up natural relations with women and were consumed with passion for one another, men committing shameless acts with men and receiving in their own persons the due penalty for their error. And since they did not see fit to acknowledge God, God gave them up to a base mind and to improper conduct. They were

filled with all manner of wickedness, evil, covetousness, malice. Full of envy, murder, strife, deceit, malignity, they are gossips, slanderers, haters of God, insolent, haughty, boastful, inventors of evil, disobedient to parents, foolish, faithless, heartless, ruthless. Though they know God's decree that those who do such things deserve to die, they not only do them but approve those who practice them.

Three times in this passage Paul says, "God gave them up." It describes what happens to us if we reject God's rule in our lives and are determined to live life our own way. It breaks God's heart when we do this, but he created us to decide for ourselves who the master of our life will be.

For those who decide to live without God, immorality and broken relationships are inevitable results. But for marriage partners whose life is built on a common faith, there is every promise of God that their love will flourish — blessing them and others as long as they live.

Being in love is exhilarating. Every joy is heightened and every blow is cushioned when you share it with someone you love. Being in love, staying in love, and growing in love comes from intelligent thought, planning, and committed action.

So many people today have not yet found the spiritual resources for such loving relationships. But these resources are available to all who seek them. They grow out of our commitment to Jesus as Lord. If your marriage is built on a solid foundation, it will not just endure; it will flourish. Your marriage can claim all those blessings that God pours out on the intimate, lifelong relationship of two lives now blended into one!

---

[1]Howard and Charlotte Clinebell, *Intimate Marriage* (New York: Harper & Row, 1970), p. 179.

# Please Listen To Me
## —Effective Communication

Chapter 6

I hurt my wife's feelings recently. The words I spoke were legitimate, and my grammar and diction were accurate. But I found out later it was the tone of my voice that hurt. When she told me I had hurt her feelings, *my* feelings were hurt because she had not understood my good intentions.

This chapter is about how to develop effective communication. It is written especially for husbands —not because husbands *cannot* communicate well but because they usually *do* not.

Husbands come home tired, frazzled, and harried from spinning around at work, and they wish for a direct "computer hook-up" with their wives to "feed" the entire day's happenings into them without having to answer one single question.

But a wife is not a computer; she has feelings. Communication skills between people are more sophisticated than those with a computer. Communication in good marriages usually take years to perfect. One authority says it takes at least thirty years to create the best marriages.

There is a desperate need for communication skills that cultivate, not kill, intimate talk in the home. More often than not, it is incompetence in communication that drives husbands and wives insane or to the divorce court, not a lack of love.

Like a surgeon's skills, good communication skills take time and hard work to develop. Unlike a skillful surgeon who operates carefully, an unskilled communicator cuts carelessly. He makes slashes until he hits the "right spot," thoughtless of the wounds and infection he leaves behind. Common sense is not enough. We must learn the skill of sensitive, accurate communication. *What* we say and *how* we say it *IS* important. Men have died for saying the wrong thing! (Prov. 18:21).

## Communication Is Life

Communication is to love what blood is to the body. When communication stops, loves begins to die. Husbands and wives should discuss goals, judge values, and analyze ambitions with total honesty and integrity, or they will never become truly married persons. They will remain married singles.

"Poor communication is the main problem in 86 percent of all troubled marriages," according to Dr. David Mace, past president of the American Association of Marriage Counselors.

Columnist Ann Landers says:

> The most important single ingredient in a marriage is the ability to communicate. If my mail is a fair reflection of what goes on with Mr. and Mrs. America behind closed doors (and I think it is), most marital problems stem from the inability of two people to talk to each other.

How precious is the ability to communicate!
... The couples who are secure in marriage
can be honest about all kinds of feelings ....

The ability to talk *and listen* is one way of measuring the effectiveness of a life. Thomas Mann believes that "speech is civilization itself." Arthur Eisenstadt says, "If our language is faulty or inefficient, then to that extent so are our lives."

## A Pattern Of Miscommunication

There is a pattern of miscommunication, which invariably leads to marriage counseling or the divorce court. The first step is a disagreement that cannot be resolved. Second, the disagreement grows into a violent argument. The third phase begins when the couple decides *they* cannot solve the argument. The last phase is one of despair, and hope is abandoned for a solution: "Why talk about it any longer? You wouldn't understand anyway." Each gives up trying to explain. Both experience the feeling of being "tried and found guilty," rather than the feeling of being listened to with understanding. Sometimes they turn to a third party for help. Hopefully, the third party will be a professional counselor, but often it is a "misunderstood" mate in another marriage — and the marriage/miscommunication/divorce cycle continues.

## In-Depth Relationships

Often people blame unhappiness in marriage on a faulty choice of mate, but really it's a faulty *adjustment* between two reasonably chosen mates. The key to relationship-in-depth is communication-in-depth. Marriage is for *growth toward* more love. As the Bible says, "The two shall *become* one flesh. (Gen. 2:24; Mark 10:8; Eph. 5:31).

Marriage is a sensitive human relationship. It is a complex mixture of feelings, attitudes, intellects, and values. A marriage takes time and commitment to a common goal to develop relationship-in-depth. Mature love comes through negotiation, acceptance, forgiveness, self-discipline, and good faith. Nothing worthwhile comes easy.

There are a few married couples who seem to move easily and gracefully into relationship-in-depth. They are unusually mature people, with great sensitivity and consideration for others, and well matched in having a great deal in common from the very start. But there are more who come to a deep relationship the hard way, through "blood and sweat and toil and tears," as Winston Churchill said in another connection. They have to achieve trust and unity through a long, determined process of working through their interpersonal conflicts. This is the hard way, but it is not a route to be despised, because what people have fought and struggled for they prize. Achievements that come easily may never be prized.[1]

## The Determining Factor

The ability to talk freely with understanding for each other seems to be the one factor, more than any other, that determines the quality of other marital ingredients. Such things as sex, raising children, recreation, in-laws, and money seem to play a secondary role. When loving communication stops, the other ingredients of marriage suffer. Jourard says, "Failure of dialogue is the crisis of our time, whether it be between nation and nation, us and them, or you and I."[2]

# Rules For Fantastic Conversation

When husbands and wives fail to understand each other, they have probably broken one or more of the following helps to fantastic conversation.

**1. Be knowledgeable.** Roots are to flowers what knowledge is to love. Without knowledge there can be no love because love grows out of knowledge.

It takes time to truly know someone; there is no shortcut. Business leaders spend thousands of dollars investigating their businesses to see where they are losing money, time, or energy. Surprisingly, these same people balk at going to a marriage enrichment seminar or workshop with their husbands or wives to learn more effective ways of living together. They refuse to spend time studying the needs, thoughts, or aspirations of their mate. It is not surprising that some are amazed to receive divorce papers. They had no idea that their marriage was even in trouble.

A Christian husband lives "*considerately* with his wife, *bestowing honor* on the woman. (1 Pet 3:7) To be considerate means to be sensitive and understanding. Understanding requires knowledge, and knowledge requires "time out" with her — time alone to talk and have a heart-to-heart sharing of the meaningful things in life. It means finding out what makes her tick. If you really *know* your wife, it is easier to love her.

Take this test to see how much "in touch" with her you are. If your wife is handy, I hope you will have her check your answers before your continue reading. If you get them *all* right, you are a super communicator *and* lover.

# HOW MUCH DO YOU KNOW ABOUT
# YOUR SPOUSE?

Instructions: The husband answers first and covers his answer. Then, the wife answers. Next, uncover the husband's answer. Compare the answers and discuss them.

|  | Wife's Answer | Husband's Answer |
|---|---|---|
| **What is your wife's favorite:** | | |
| 1. food? | _____ | _____ |
| 2. drink? | _____ | _____ |
| 3. place to eat? | _____ | _____ |
| 4. dress? | _____ | _____ |
| 5. tv program? | _____ | _____ |
| 6. tv entertainer? | _____ | _____ |
| 7. movie personality? | _____ | _____ |
| 8. shoes? | _____ | _____ |
| 9. room in the house? | _____ | _____ |
| 10. chair? | _____ | _____ |
| 11. U.S. president (of the last three)? | _____ | _____ |
| 12. book? | _____ | _____ |
| 13. magazine? | _____ | _____ |
| 14. sport? | _____ | _____ |
| 15. hobby? | _____ | _____ |
| 16. song? | _____ | _____ |

17. composer? _____ _____

18. flower? _____ _____

19. color? _____ _____

20. animal? _____ _____

21. car? _____ _____

22. friend? _____ _____

23. brand of makeup? _____ _____

24. candy? _____ _____

25. toothpaste? _____ _____

26. kind of vacation? _____ _____

27. way to spend
evenings? _____ _____

28. perfume? _____ _____

2. **Be loving.** Anyone can carry on a beautiful relationship when his or her spouse is doing all the right things. But when the spouse does all the wrong things, it's another matter. Great sex can help for a while, but it takes sacrificial love to surmount ugly things that arise in most of our spouses. A love that

is patient and kind; . . . is not jealous or conceited . . . or proud; . . . not ill-mannered, or selfish, or irritable; does not keep a record of wrongs; is not happy with evil, but is happy with the truth. . . never gives up: its faith, hope, and patience never fail. . . is eternal . . . .

1 Corinthians 13:4-8, TEV

It takes a lot of dying to self to create this kind of love. It isn't easy to forgive someone who abuses you verbally or physically, but this is what Jesus taught us to do. Those who want to bail out of marriage when they find faults in their partner will keep divorcing and remarrying in a vain attempt to find a spouse with no sin. A better way is acceptance, unconditional love, grace, and forgiveness. When partners exchange grace and forgiveness, they grow closer to each other and God.

Christianity doesn't say to love your married partner *if* you *feel* good about him or her, but to *do* good whether you feel like it or not. No marriage will last very long if the partners return evil for evil. They must learn to receive a negative and give a positive.

Shortly after I hurt my wife's feelings that day, I was sitting in "my" chair reading when she came to me with a sandwich and a glass of orange juice. I couldn't read or eat until I made things right. Her loving actions (when she had a " right" to resent me) "forced" me to make up. No words from her could have restored our relationship so quickly.

3. **Be transparent.** A window lets light shine through and allows us to see what otherwise might be hidden. Truth, according to Heidegger, is ". . . when what is hidden is no longer so." Scripture admonishes us to "speak the truth, in love." This is what transparency is about — truth.

It is unwise in inter-personal relations to share our innermost thoughts indiscriminately, but it is a tragedy not to share them with the person we have chosen for life. I know Ann Landers and her sister disagree with me. They think that "what the other person does not know will not hurt them." I think Christians are privileged to look deeper and more profoundly into each other because the Holy Spirit enables them to act graciously toward any ugliness that truth might uncover. The ideal is the transparent nakedness of Adam and Eve before sin entered the world.

Women seem to naturally crave this deep relationship more than men. But the need for transparency is present whether we are aware of it or not. The reason is obvious: to deeply love is to deeply know. "Yes," some reply, "but I'm afraid to share deeply because if I tell you who I really am, you might not like me — and me is all I've got." But this doesn't have to happen, especially to Christian couples. While uncovering areas of ugliness to each other, we "test the water" to see if the other is ready for more revelation. Timing is important. We gradually reveal ourselves. Our mates should receive such things with a forgiving spirit because, as Christians, they have received the mercy of God themselves. Also, sharing this information is a compliment and an expression of love and confidence in a trustworthy partner.

I have been truthful with my wife, except for one thing I kept secret. I was afraid to share this one thing for fear it would damage her self-image. During a Marriage Encounter weekend I carefully and tenderly shared this last secret with her. My secret was written in loving detail. My anxiety rose with every sentence she read. When she finished, she look at me with loving self-confidence and said,"This is no problem to me at all." I had used tons of emotional energy for seventeen years keeping this from her, and she handled it beautifully in seventeen seconds! What a waste of emotional energy! What a waste of time we could have spent together! And I found an unexpected joy — I had more confidence in her capacity to receive and share my feelings both positive and negative. My fear of hurting her was gone. We could be more "one" than I had imagined possible.

A choice that confronts everyone of us at every moment is this: shall we permit our fellow men to know us as we now are, or shall we seek instead to remain an enigma, an uncertain quantity wishing to be seen as something we are not. When we are not truly known by the other people in our lives, we are misunderstood. When we are not known, even by family and friends, we join the all too numerous "lonely crowd."

Worse, when we succeed too well in hiding our being from others, we tend to lose touch with our real selves, and this loss of self contributes to illness in its many forms.[3]

Dr. David Mace, past president of the American Association of Marriage and Family Counselors, said:

There may be a few rare situations in which husband and wife may legitimately withhold the truth from one another; but it is my view that this inevitably involves a misfortune. To have to censor your communication to your marriage partner and close off a portion of your thoughts that cannot be shared is fatal to the achievement of relationship-in-depth.[4]

Dr. Mace says marriage is a "complete pooling of possessions and the entering into a joint life, face to face, with nothing reserved or held back. Anything less than that is only a partial marriage . . These couples will never know the meaning of relationship-in-depth."

4. **Be trustworthy.** A husband or wife must trust the other and develop confidence, faith, and hope. There is no room for suspicion or doubt.

Sometimes there is no time for full explanation or clarification because the show must go on. Only deep underlying trust in each other will keep the ship on an even keel at such times. If such trust does not exist, there will almost inevitably be mutual recrimination and quarrels and arguments. . . .[5]

Each partner must be careful to never arouse legitimate suspicion. According to James Othuis, if marriage partners do not consider their relationship a permanent trust for life,

they will live in permanent crisis. . .Marriage has to be a betrothal for life, or the partners will never be able to tolerate quarreling, arguing, sulking, mistakes, disagreements, or even the mildest criticism.[6]

5. **Be positive.** A marriage that is 85 percent positive and only 15 percent negative will appear 90 percent bad if the couple spends 90 percent of its time arguing over the 15 percent problem areas. Never spend more time on a problem area than what it deserves, nor allow minor differences to dominate too much time. Maximize the positive—minimize the negative. One writer said, "Define what is important and stress it; define what is unimportant and ignore it."

6. **Be sensitive.** Most men speak from the head more than from the heart. With women it is usually the other way around. This poses a problem.

The head level usually deals with things: concepts, ideas, philosophy, judgments, or facts. The heart level deals with emotions: joy, love, lumps in the throat, tears, fears, hurts, and emptiness of the heart. In general, men do not deal well with this "feeling" level of communication. This is regrettable because a person (man or woman) is more nearly defined by what he *feels* than by what he *thinks*. Hurts, fears, and emotions are especially important to wives because women are very sensitive. They really don't think they can fully know their husbands or deeply love them until they know their hearts.

Also, feelings themselves are neither right nor wrong, good nor bad — they are just feelings. Feelings *happen* to us. Guilt doesn't lie in *having* a feeling, but in what you *do* with the feeling. To say, "You shouldn't *feel* that way," or "you *know* better than that," doesn't change the feeling. What we need is someone to *understand* the feeling, not someone to *judge* the feeling. It is amazing how an understanding mate can help make bad feelings quickly disappear. Accept all feelings (good and bad) and try to understand them. Your spouse will love you for it.

7. **Be an effective communicator.** Three little old ladies were traveling on a train in England. One said, "Is this Wimberly?" Another responded, "No, this is Thursday." The third lady said, "I am too; let's get a drink."

I understand what I am saying, so I assume that others hear my words exactly as I do. The word "fast," for example, has several meanings, as does "hot," "cool," and "baby." Because of different uses of words (tonal inflection, body language, preconceived ideas, and other non-verbal distortions), it is easy for a spouse to interpret what is said differently from the intended meaning.

To become an effective communicator, you must closely observe your listener. Slight clues are often enough reason to stop and check out what the other is receiving. "What did you hear me say just now?" "I get the feeling I'm not coming through just right."

8. **Be an active listener.** Our culture is built on talk — not conversation. Television talks to us con-

95

stantly. We are talked to on the job, at school, and at church. Newspapers, magazines, and books "talk" to us. People around us usually enjoy talking more than listening. Where are the listeners? Some neurotics simply give up and start talking to themselves.

The Christian knows God is the greatest of listeners: ". . . they shall call on my name, and I will hear them" (Zech. 13:9, KJV). Jesus listened attentively to anyone — the downtrodden, the sinful, the rich, the poor, and the righteous. Often he said, "He who has ears, let him hear . . ." (Matt. 13:9, 43). The word "hear" is used more than 1,300 times in the Bible.

The Pharisee and the Sadducee of Jesus' day heard sounds, but they didn't listen: "hearing, they do not hear" (Matt. 13:13). Their inner ears were closed by their preconceived views, resulting in the crucifixion.

---

### "A good listener learns to listen to what is not said . . . ."

---

"A wise man will hear, and will increase learning" (Prov. 1:5, KJV). Listen thoroughly to the *whole* story; don't jump to conclusions. "He who states his case first seems right, until the other comes and examines him" (Prov. 18:17). We must hear *completely:* "If one gives answer *before he hears,* it is his folly and shame" (Prov. 18:13). This may be why Jesus wants us to be quick to hear and slow to speak (James 1:19, Prov. 29:20). Good listeners bring life into dead relationships.

Arthur Eisenstadt describes what he calls the "creative listener":

He, by his attentive manner, his approving mien and his overt signals of interest, appreciation and respect, stimulates and encourages the communicator to greater heights of self-expression, fluency and enthusiasm.[7]

A good listener learns to listen to what is *not* said, to the "edges" of the conversation and hidden meanings. Rogers, a noted psychologist, puts it this way:

A number of times in my life I have felt myself bursting with insoluble problems, or going round and round in tormented circles or, during one period, overcome by feelings of worthlessness and despair . . . I have been able to find individuals who have been able to hear me and thus to rescue me from the chaos of my feelings . . . who have been able to hear my meanings a little more deeply than I have known them . . . I can testify that when you are in psychological stress and someone really hears you without passing judgment on you, without trying to take responsibility for you, without trying to mold you, it feels good . . . It has permitted me to bring out the frightening feelings, the guilts, the despair, the confusions . . . It is astonishing how elements which seem insoluble become soluble when someone listens. How confusions which seemed irremediable turn into relatively clear flow-streams when one is heard.[8]

9. **Be concise.** Bacon said, "Writing maketh an exact man." Writing forces you to read what you've written, rethink it, and then rewrite it. It makes you concise. Many of the sweetest and kindest oral statements have been lost forever. Feelings *in writing,* like cards, letters, and thank-you notes to your spouse, are special communications. Wives know this, and husbands need to learn it.

Writing is almost a necessity if arguments develop in a marriage. Words fly fast, hard feelings dominate, and a verbal battle follows. There are five reasons for writing negative thoughts before speaking them. First, the emotional heat usually cools off during the writing time. Second, each spouse is able to *finish* the entire thought without fear of being interrupted. Third, when the partner reads the letter he is forced to receive the entire message before answering. Fourth, writing forces the critical writer to see his harsh, critical feelings in cold print. Usually, as the letter progresses, hard feelings phase out and good feelings surface. Often, when one spouse is not verbally articulate, the other tends to dominate the conversation. Fifth, writing gives the non-verbal spouse an equal amount of time.

10. **Be prayerful.** People often ask me, "What one single thing do you recommend, more than any other, to make marriage communication beautiful?" My answer: conversational prayer. Prayer gives insights into God and your spouse that you get no other way. In prayer, you see the throbbing heart, the philosophy, and the cares. The troubles of your marriage are laid bare before God. Couple-prayer is meaningful conversation between a couple addressed to God. It takes a duet and makes it a trio. In prayer, God's spirit is injected; hurts are healed and forgiveness is granted. Nothing compares with it. You can't fully benefit from prayer unless you try it regularly over a long period of time.

11. **Be decisive.** You will never *find* time to talk, write, communicate, or pray. You must *make* time. Decide that your marriage will be top priority in your lives. Decide that the two of you will take whatever time is necessary to make it happen.

# Barriers To Great Communication

Some barriers to communication are purely *mechanical*, like distance, volume, speech, or hearing problems. These are usually called external barriers.

There are also *internal or psychological* barriers that hamper communication. Words full of emotion may color the message or cloud the tone, and they usually invite emotional reactions which are not conducive to effective communication. On the other hand, emotions locked in and kept silent also set up barriers to communication.

There are also *intellectual* barriers. Inaccurate analysis of data, fallacious reasoning, disorganized thought or expression, and premature conclusions all lead to ineffective conversation. Most people do not think before they speak. The mouth tends to be in gear before the brain starts, and listeners tend to hold the speaker accountable for what he said, not for what he *intended* to say. Also, many times a decision is stated too quickly. The listener reacts negatively to a premature conclusion. A speaker needs to give the reason for a decision *before* he shares the decision.

The following is a list of "barriers to communication" that will impede or absolutely stop good conversation between husband and wife. Avoid them at all cost.

**1. Materialism.** Materialism is simply putting things before people. When he was trying to tempt Christ, Satan said, " . . . To you I will give all this authority and their glory" (Luke 4:6). Authority and glory seem like useful tools to accomplish much good, but Jesus' kingdom was established by the poor and his authority was derived from the cross, not Wall Street.

Wives, children, and husbands need people more than things. A woman craves her husband's *time* more than the extra money he makes working overtime. Children want Dad's and Mom's time more than their gifts. A man wants his wife's attention more than a spotless house.

The human person is the greatest of all creations. Honoring the person is honoring God, who designed and brought into being the person as the peak of His creation. In our materialistic world, there is a continually lurking danger of letting concern for money and the things money can buy outrank the persons of the family in one's talk, in one's desires and in one's attention.[9]

2. **Critical attitude.** Psychologist Carl Rogers believes that "the major barrier to mutual interpersonal communication is our very natural tendency to judge, to evaluate, to approve (or disapprove) the statements of the other person or the other group."[10] Life with a fault-finder is misery. Our spouses are to love, not to criticize. The critical person is highly judgmental and feels qualified to read your mind. He judges one single feeling as your complete motivation. He interrupts and uses flare words (words he knows will arouse hard feelings). Sarcasm is another of his characteristics. Sometimes his critical nature reveals itself in pouting silence; at other times, it comes out in a shout.

Sometimes intense inferiority feelings will cause critical attitudes. We cut others "down to our size" so we will not feel so inadequate. Whatever its cause, a negative, critical attitude should be the first barrier torn down. Jesus teaches us to handle the critical spirit through prayer, not through retaliation (Matt. 5:44). To those who tend to judge, Jesus says *stop* and examine your own life: " . . . first take the log out of your own eye" (Matt. 7:1-5).

**3. Fear.** When a husband frequently judges or criticizes his wife, she is afraid to be open or reveal her inner self. On the other hand, if the wife can't take *any* negatives without turning on the tears, her husband will be afraid of hurting her and will not speak from his heart. Fear, then, is present on both sides. Fear freezes communication. Couples need to share their weaknesses, temptations, sins, needs, dreams, negative feelings, and even crazy ideas. Hopefully, fear is avoided and confidence is created so the "real me" is known and loved.

**4. Manipulation.** No one is comfortable if he feels he is being manipulated. Nagging, whining, pouting, bargaining, being gushy, lying, and switching the subject are a few methods used to motivate a person to think *my* way *without his knowing it*. This might work occasionally, but resentment follows after it is discovered. It creates continual mistrust and defensiveness.

**5. Preoccupation.** Our American culture is filled with so many *urgent* activities that we have very little time for the *important* ones. It is a matter of priorities. Most of us attend to the urgent things first, like the telephone, car pool, appointments, scouts, meals, schooling, chorus practice, music lessons, ball games, ad infinitum. When we get through with these things that "have to be done," we find no time for the *important* things, such as Bible reading, prayer, devotion, quiet time, and developing an intense personal relationship with Christ, spouse, and children.

One solution is to list all the things on paper that need to be done each day (or week). Establish priorities by putting the most *important* items at the head of the list and the least toward the end. Then, start from the top. You will probably never complete all the

101

items, but you will have the fantastic satisfaction of knowing that you always do the most important things every day.

6. **Dullness.** Dullness captivates the marriage that does not try new things: different foods, eating places, wall paper, carpet, paint, ideas, jokes, books, magazines. Every time you see a happy, vibrant marriage (no matter how long they have been married), chances are they are growing through trying new things together, learning new things, talking about new ideas, and experimenting. God gave us creativity and expects us to use it.

7. **Alcohol.** Don't let the sparkle and the smooth taste of strong wine deceive you (Prov. 23:31-32). Drinking alcohol slows speech and makes conversation difficult. But the drinker *thinks* he is a great conversationalist. From a psychological standpoint, alcohol clouds the super ego (the conscience or value system). O.H. Mowrer, past president of the American Psychological Association, calls alcohol a "super ego solvent." The drinker loses part of his value system, and if he continues to drink, he next loses his decision-making skills. That is why drinkers who drive are such a risk on the highways. Good conversation is one of many things in a marriage ruined by drinking.

8. **Dishonesty.** Good marriages are characterized by honesty and truth. When a husband and wife cannot be honest with each other, major problems occur. " . . . A poor man is better than a liar" (Prov. 19:22). The problem must be remedied, or the marriage is in danger. Consistent lying is a major character fault, and professional counseling is needed immediately. The problem with the liar is that he, like the alcohol user, seldom admits to having a problem. But transparent honesty is a must according to David Mace:

When two people live as close to one another as husband and wife do, it is impossible to maintain mutual trust without transparent honesty. Lack of honesty leads to lack of understanding, which creates suspicion, resentment, and hostility.[11]

## How To Argue Fairly

In marital relations and in physics, heat destroys. Paul said, "Have nothing to do with stupid, senseless controversies; you know that they breed quarrels" (2 Tim. 2:23). He also said "to speak evil of no one, to avoid quarreling. . ."(Titus 3:2). But God knew that we would get into arguments because Christ recommends that when we have controversy, we should agree with our adversary quickly (Matt. 5:25). When you find yourself in an argument, how do you argue fairly?

1. **Clarify the issue.** Make sure you know what the issue is. Often arguments are solved before they start by being sure the people involved are not arguing about two different issues.

2. **Repeat their words.** Check out your assumptions. Repeat, in different words but as precisely as possible, what your partner has just said to you. Sound simple? Try it — you might be surprised. Your partner will often exclaim, "That is not what I said." When this happens, have your spouse say it again. This time, listen more carefully. Then, try repeating once more what you think was said. Many arguments are solved when one understands exactly what the other has said.

3. **Choose the right time.** Arguments that pop up at the wrong time (like 3 o'clock in the morning) are unwise to follow up. This is one time procrastination pays off. Learn to put a discussion or fuss off until there is no unnerving inconvenience.

4. **Look before you leap.** Often, after an argument,

103

we look back and see no real accomplishment. If the goal is not worth the risk, concede before you start. "The beginning of strife is like letting out water; so quit before the quarrel breaks out" (Prov. 17:14).

**5. Resolve to resolve.** "Sixty-eight percent of both husbands and wives say that disagreements are seldom resolved."[12] Too often we start arguing about one issue and then get into a mud-throwing contest over ten side issues without resolving any one of them. If you have agreed on an issue which needs to be discussed, then stay on that *one* subject.

**6. Attack the problem, not the person.** When arguments turn into mud-throwing contests, usually someone feels he is losing ground and resorts to a mud ball to equal things up. Mud-throwing contests are seldom equal. Someone puts a rock in his or her mud ball — and the marriage has had it. Mud slinging usually begins with a statement like: "What you are saying about me is no worse than when you . . . ." Here comes the mud! It's usually unfair to dig up the past. Leave it buried.

**7. Hold hands.** Silly, but it works. You will never know how hard it is to argue holding hands until you have tried it. This non-verbal communication (holding hands) says, "I love you and want to hold you." It is impossible to verbally assault your mate while holding hands. You will either drop your hands and "reach for a mud ball," or you will tone down your argument and resolve it. One couple told me, "We have gotten really frustrated, angry, scared, and tearful; *but* instead of 'fussing and fighting it out' as we have done so often, we took hands and 'prayed it out.' What a difference this made." Try it — and don't turn loose until you have prayed.

## Some Final Reminders About Conflict

Conflict is common to all sinners. The question is how to deal with it. David Mace says:

> Two people living so close together cannot expect to be in agreement all the time about everything. They are the products of different backgrounds, and they have consequently learned to approach the business of living in different ways — each has his own method, his own order of priority, his own pace. Thrown together in a common task, they will inevitably clash. And the business of marriage is to work on the differences that arise, analyze them, understand and respect each other's sincerity and good will, work out compromise adjustments; and then tackle the slow, discouraging task of changing habit patterns in order to achieve more harmonious cooperation. There is no easy way to do this. There are no shortcuts, no labor saving gimmicks. It can be done only when two people have the resolute will to do it, because the goal is sufficiently important to them both.[13]

Conflict should be dealt with openly. Suppression builds tension and resentment, elevating the intensity of the conflict.

Most arguments are only symptoms of a deeper issue. For example, when a fuss erupts over an overdrawn checking account, is the real issue the $3.00 charge for the bad check or the insulting way your spouse "puts you down" for not "having more sense"? Most likely, it's a wounded ego that is the real issue. We need love. And when we feel unloved or rebuked, we fight over the least issues. Look for the underlying problems, solve them, and be surprised how the conflicts diminish.

Arguments conducted fairly clear the air and make room for growth. There is no growth while partners hold grudges and resentments. Jesus himself confronted people at times (Mark 9:11-19; 10:13-15; Matt. 5:23-24; 18:16-17). He cleaned "the air" as well as the temple.

Arguments can be resolved best after we first commit ourselves to each other for life.

> Marriage has to be a betrothal for life, or the partners will never be able to tolerate quarreling, arguing, sulking, mistakes, disagreements, or even the mildest criticism. All conflicts become traumatic experiences, for over every quarrel hangs these unsettling questions: Do I want to divorce now? Does she want out? Is he trying to get rid of me? ... Only couples who pledge their troth for life have the freedom to develop their marriage as they should.[14]

## Communications Test

Insert your spouse's name in the blank space and answer the questions as you think your spouse sees you. The wife answers first and covers her answer. The husband answers next. Then, take an hour together to talk about the answers.

Does _____ think you:

|  | Husband | Wife |
|---|---|---|
| 1. are considerate of others' feelings? | Yes No | Yes No |
| 2. allow money or things to spoil human relationships? | Yes No | Yes No |

3. share how much you need him/her?      Yes No    Yes No

4. read enough on the subject of husband/wife relations?    Yes No    Yes No

5. endeavor to make your sexual relationships more sensitive and meaningful?    Yes No    Yes No

6. talk excessively?      Yes No    Yes No

7. do not share enough of your inner feelings?    Yes No    Yes No

8. use too many words or phrases that are too easily misunderstood?    Yes No    Yes No

9. have an overly critical attitude?    Yes No    Yes No

10. have too much tendency to speak *for* the other person?    Yes No    Yes No

11. have a tendency to interrupt another person?    Yes No    Yes No

12. use too many words that belittle others?    Yes No    Yes No

13. change the subject too often when the subject gets too uncomfortable for you? Or does he/she think you won't even bring it up?    Yes No    Yes No

14. nag too often?    Yes No    Yes No

15. have trouble looking others in the eye?    Yes No    Yes No

16. choose "peace" over sharing honest feelings?  Yes No  Yes No

17. make too many excuses?  Yes No  Yes No

18. clam up too often?  Yes No  Yes No

19. watch too much tv?  Yes No  Yes No

20. read too much when home?  Yes No  Yes No

21. are "off somewhere" (day-dreaming) when he/she is talking to you?  Yes No  Yes No

22. are sensitive when he/she is discouraged, troubled, or hurt?  Yes No  Yes No

23. are complimentary often enough?  Yes No  Yes No

24. criticize him/her too often?  Yes No  Yes No

25. are sarcastic too often?  Yes No  Yes No

26. honestly try to see another person's point of view?  Yes No  Yes No

27. honestly enjoy listening to another's point of view?  Yes No  Yes No

28. monopolize too much of the conversation?  Yes No  Yes No

29. encourage others to share their thoughts and feelings?  Yes No  Yes No

30. speak the truth in a loving manner?  Yes No  Yes No

31. get too upset when others
disagree with you?      Yes No    Yes No

32. share so little of yourself
that others cannot get to
know you?      Yes No    Yes No

---

[1]David Mace, "Marriage as Relationship-in-Depth," *Marital Therapy*, ed. H.L. Silverman (Springfield: Charles C. Thomas, 1972), p. 163.

[2]Sidney Jourard, "Marriage Is For Life," *Journal of Marriage and Family Counseling*, p. 199.

[3]Jourard, p. 199.

[4]Mace, p. 164.

[5]Mace, p. 167.

[6]James Othuis, *I Pledge You My Troth* (New York: Harper and Row, 1975), p. 40.

[7]Arthur Eisenstadt, "Language and Communication in Marriage Counseling," *Marital Counseling*, ed. H.L. Silverman (Springfield: Charles C. Thomas, 1967).

[8]Carl Rogers, "Some Elements of Effective Interpersonal Communication," (a talk given at California Institute of Technology, Pasadena, Calif., Nov. 9, 1964, p. 4), in *Listening as a Way of Becoming*, ed. Carl Koile (Waco: Word, 1977), p. 129.

[9]Gordon Lester, "Home Backgrounds for Sex Instruction," *Marital Counseling*, ed. H.L. Silverman (Springfield: Charles C. Thomas, 1967), p. 19.

[10]Carl Rogers and F.J. Roethsliberger, "Barriers and Gateways to Communication," *Harvard Business Review*, XX (July-August 1962), p. 19.

[11]Mace, p. 164.

[12]Wilfred Abse, Ethel Nash, Lois Louden, *Marital and Sexual Counseling in Medical Practice* (New York: Harper and Row, 1974), p. 115.

[13]Mace, p. 167.

[14]Philip Yancey, "Marriage: Minefields on the Way to Paradise," in *Christianity Today*, p. 24.

# I Want To Hold You
## – Sexual Intimacy

### Chapter 7

A funny thing happened to sex on its way to the twentieth century. It lost its good reputation.

Modern generations treat sex as though it were the product of some modern, wicked, pornographic mind. It is not. God created sex, and he created it for man's good. Man has taken this aspect of God's creation, like everything else, and perverted it.

God's original design was "male" and "female." Each of us is indelibly stamped with one or the other of those genetic codes. And our sexuality influences virtually everything we do. It is, therefore, extremely important that we understand the nature of our human sexuality. In doing so, we learn to fulfil in our lives the promise and potential for which we were created.

## Becoming One Flesh

In the beginning, when the Creator had created everything except woman, the Lord God said, "It is not good that the man should be alone; I will make him a helper fit for him" (Gen. 2:18). But before he created Eve, God presented to Adam every animal. But among the animals there was not found a suitable partner for man (Gen. 2:20).

Now, that is interesting. It is interesting that God would present every animal in existence to the man as a potential partner. God knew that there was as yet no partner "fit" to share man's life. But God wanted Adam to know it. He wanted Adam to look over every possible partner and realize that a suitable partner was not yet available among all of God's creation.

Then, God created woman and presented her to man (Gen. 2:22). There she was, fresh from the hand of God, designed especially to share man's life. And part of that sharing was sexual: ". . . God blessed them, and God said to them, 'Be fruitful and multiply . . . ' " (Gen. 1:28). And again the Lord said, "Therefore a man leaves his father and his mother and cleaves to his wife, and they become one flesh" (Gen. 2:24). That "one flesh" is more comprehensive than the sexual relationship, but sex is a very basic part of that which is included.

## A Gift to Celebrate

In the New Testament, Hebrews 13:4 says, "Let marriage be held in honor among all, and let the marriage bed be undefiled; for God will judge the immoral and adulterous." That word translated "bed" could also be translated "coitus." That's what it is talking about. The inspired writer is saying that the sexual relationship between husband and wife is a holy, sacred, God-given relationship. Husbands and wives should *celebrate* that fact!

Then, there is the passage that holds up sexual love as an ideal: "that each one of you know how to

111

take a wife for himself in holiness and honor, not in the passion of lust like heathen who do not know God" (1 Thess. 4:4-5).

Too many marriages today are based primarily on sexual attraction. What used to be a search for a marriage partner is more and more a search for a sexual partner. But Paul is telling us that a partner is more than that. This prospective partner is a complete human being with a full range of potential. There is much more to look for in a relationship than the sexual part. Focusing too heavily on the sexual aspects of the relationship risks ignoring the larger potential of a full partnership.

Paul describes what sex can be like when it is based on a full and complete relationship. Paul writes:

> But because of the temptation to immorality, each man should have his own wife and each woman her own husband. The husband should give to his wife her conjugal rights, and likewise the wife to her husband. For the wife does not rule over her own body, but the husband does; likewise the husband does not rule over his own body, but the wife does. Do not refuse one another except perhaps by agreement for a season, that you may devote yourselves to prayer; but then come together again, lest Satan tempt you through lack of self-control.
>
> 1 Corinthians 7:2-5

Notice first of all that Paul does not mention procreation at all in this passage. Having babies is a legitimate function of the sexual part of marriage. But it is not the exclusive function of the relationship. A moral relationship cannot be achieved without regular and (for most) fairly frequent sexual satisfaction.

Notice, also, Paul says that in marriage, each gives his own body to the other (vs. 4). Such a gift is an extremely important trust, to be accepted lovingly and never abused. In marriage, neither partner rules any longer over his or her own body. The partner is now lovingly given that privilege.

Then Paul says, "Do not refuse one another . . . (vs. 5). What a strong, all-encompassing command. Both the King James Version and the American Standard Version translate, "Defraud ye not one the other. . . ." Strong language! But it is such an important consideration that the inspired writer included it so there would be no misunderstanding.

Problems develop over the withholding of sexual satisfaction: hostility, resentment, and bitterness. These are poisons which contaminate the marriage. Love learns to respond to emotional and sexual needs and to help the relationship grow.

The sexual relationship between a husband and wife is the only one that can allow two people to be completely open with each other while totally involved with each other.

## The Greatest Honor

To be asked to spend one's life together with another person is one of the greatest honors in life. And one of the greatest honors we can bestow on another is to make, with that person, a lifelong commitment of marriage.

How much greater that honor is if both people have saved for each other the special experience of sexual relations. Sex is the greatest honor of all — if this experience is one which neither has ever experienced with another; if it is a special experience which each has to share for a lifetime with that special person; and if, in marriage, each vows never to share this experience with any other person ever.

To share this experience with someone outside the marriage relationship robs it of its power to honor. The more it is shared outside marriage, the more common it becomes. This commonness erodes the deeper meaning, since those with whom it is shared cannot really be all that unique.

God has given each of us a priceless gift. It is a gift given to us to give away. It is to be saved for one very special person — that person with whom we choose to share the rest of life. God intended for us to treasure the gift because of its unique power to honor another.

## One of a Kind

Sexual union should never be viewed without the larger context of the relationship. Sexual union without the marriage commitment of a lifetime together is immoral — it is destructive.

This fact should tell us something about God's design for the relationship. Each of us needs another person who will share life in a completely unique way — in a way that we share life with no other. Because God made us so, each of us needs to be "one of a kind" to another human being.

By reserving the sexual union experience for one person only, we do become one of a kind to each other. Husband and wife who share the sexual experience with each other, but with no one else during their entire life, achieve a precious uniqueness that others can scarcely imagine.

Such a commitment allows one relationship in life to achieve its full potential. In contrast, sexual relationships outside the larger context rob intimacy of its basic purpose and meaning.

I believe that God intended the sexual relationship to be a joyous celebration of another day of loving and sharing of life together. It enables a husband

and a wife to say to each other, "I love you ecstatically and enjoy immensely our shared life."

If that is what the sexual relationship is in marriage, two people must have something to celebrate in order for sex to be really meaningful. They celebrate that which is central to their marriage: commitment, love, companionship, caring, and sharing. This is what gives sex its real meaning. Two people must focus their attention on the centralities if their sexual relationship is to achieve its full potential.

## Ten Suggestions for Husbands

Over the years, I have developed "Ten Suggestions for Husbands" and "Ten Suggestions for Wives," which have to do specifically with enhancing the sexual part of their life together. Let's begin with "Ten Suggestions for Husbands":

1. **Tell her you love her every day and mean it.** Proverbs 27:5 says, "Better is open rebuke than hidden love." Many people love others but never express it. In the marriage relationship, it is extremely important for each to express his love for the other regularly and verbally.

2. **Never pass up an opportunity to give her sincere praise.** Every person needs sincere praise on a regular basis. We are encouraged by praise from others. It enriches our lives and makes us feel better about ourselves and all of our relationships.

3. **Always speak to others of her in a complimentary way.** This is part of loyalty. I should feel free to confess any of my faults to others, but I should never reveal the faults of my partner to others. It is my partner's responsibility to reveal her own faults; and when I reveal her faults, I am acting presumptuously.

4. **Communicate, but don't criticize.** All of us need to learn the art of effective communication.

One important lesson involves communicating clearly without hurting each other. Both husbands and wives need to learn to communicate clearly without damaging the relationship. I should feel free to let my partner know when something is making me uncomfortable or ill at ease or when something is hurting our relationship. But when I turn that communication into criticism of my partner, it harms our relationship. There is surely such a thing as constructive ciriticism, but most criticism in most marriages proves destructive. Most marriages would improve significantly if partners simply stopped criticizing altogether.

5. **Keep the spirit of courtship and romance alive in your marriage.** Husbands and wives should want to continue the courtship aspect of their relationship. It seems that most men believe they are not naturally inclined toward being romantic. Most men, in fact, feel embarrassed by romantic activities throughout their lives. Even so, I believe a man who wants to be a good husband should develop his capacity to act romantically toward his wife.

The very idea is often threatening to many husbands. Their first response is, "What do you mean 'romantic'?" My answer to this is, "Anything your wife thinks is romantic is romantic." That may sound terribly simple, but it is nevertheless true.

---

*"... romantic communication and sexual response are inevitably tied together in a marriage relationship."*

---

A lot of wives like surprises that are gift-wrapped. They like flowers, and one flower is often more romantic than a dozen. Wives like to get letters that are stamped, mailed, and brought by the mailman.

The insensitive husband cannot see why he should mail his wife a letter when he is going home and can carry it. He doesn't see why he should write her a letter if he is going home and will be talking to her later in the day. What escapes him is the romance of receiving a love letter. Yet, once started, he can often write things he is hesitant to say to her in person. By writing them and mailing them to her, he allows her a moment of surprise when she finds his letter in the mail. She has plenty of time to read the letter and to luxuriate in its warm words of love and appreciation. Later in the day, his homecoming will be enhanced; and the occasion becomes a precious memory that will return again and again to bless their relationship.

I am convinced that romantic communication and sexual response are inevitably tied together in a marriage relationship. Anytime one partner refuses to communicate, especially in a romantic way, the other partner's sexual response is partly blocked. And anytime one partner makes a sexual move and the other person is hesitant or negative, the communication gap widens. Gradually these experiences add up to impede the growth of the marriage relationship. They will keep it from becoming all marriage is meant to be.

6. **Take plenty of time for sex.** The husband is often goal-oriented. He tends to rush through the sexual experience. He's ready to go on to something else, leaving his wife tense, angry, and unsatisfied. Some studies indicate that it takes a wife an average of twenty minutes to gain full satisfaction from a sexual encounter.

7. **Discover the areas of her body which are particularly pleasurable to her.** Every wife is physically unique and continually changing. The areas of

her body which are more pleasurable today may be less pleasurable tomorrow or next week. What gives her pleasure on one occasion will not necessarily give her pleasure later. Continued learning can bring improved satisfaction in these intimate experiences.

8. **Be careful of your cleanliness and personal hygiene.** It is extremely important that both partners be clean for their intimate encounter. Body odors can be extremely offensive, and poor hygiene can be unhealthy or even dangerous.

9. **Remember that your wife cannot respond as she and you would like when her feelings are hurt, when the setting is inappropriate, or when the children are stirring in the next room.** One of the significant differences between husbands and wives has to do with the right times for sex. Husbands often believe that problems can best be solved by going to bed. Wives may feel that an invitation to go to bed with her husband is insulting and degrading if serious problems are still unresolved. Wives also tend to feel threatened by the possiblility of interruption. The purchase of a lock for the bedroom door may be a wise investment for many marriages.

10. **Communicate to her what she means to you.** She is not just "baggage," not just an extension of your personality, nor just someone you occasionally enjoy having around for your own personal satisfaction. She is your partner, friend, and lifelong lover. And she has a constant need to know that she is needed.

I remember some months ago counseling with a man whose marriage had not reached the potential that he and his wife wanted it to achieve. As we discussed the display of affection in the marriage, he said, "I didn't grow up in that kind of home. I'm not comfortable with an open display of affection."

118

I gave him an assignment. I said, "Every time you pass your wife or she passes you in the home say to her, 'You look like you need a hug.' Then take her in your arms and hug her lovingly." His reply was, "I just can't do that. I'm too uncomfortable with that kind of thing."

I reminded him of Proverb 27:5: "Better is open rebuke than hidden love." I repeated the assignment: "Take her in your arms and tell her you love her."

He said, "If I did that she would faint!" I replied, "Good! You would already have her in your arms, and you could keep her from hurting herself when she falls to the floor. Stay right there until she comes to; then hug her again, and continue the process until she becomes sufficiently accustomed to it that she will not faint when you hug her."

He laughed nervously and said, "If I did that, she would know you told me to." I replied, "If that is the best you can do for the moment, just before you take her in your arms, tell her, 'Carl told me to do this.' She will appreciate the hug regardless of why it is done."

All of us need to know that we are important to other people. Husbands and wives need to know that they are exceedingly important to each other. And so, they need to tell each other.

## Ten Suggestions for Wives

Now let's look at the "Ten Suggestions for Wives":

1. **Keep personal attractiveness at its very best.** Wives need to remember that husbands are especially "visually" oriented. What husbands see is extremely important to them. (Wives respond to this one by saying, "Tell the men that they need to keep their personal attractiveness at its very best, too.") Husbands take note.

2. **Be careful to be clean and to take care of personal hygiene.** Wives are probably more inclined to be aware of body odors than are husbands, but both should be extremely careful of this point. Intimacy can be violated by offensive odors.

3. **Take extended time for lovemaking away from all distractions.** Children, television, telephone, even mind-wandering can violate the needs of the moment. Of course, there is nothing wrong occasionally with "quick sex." But this need not be the norm for a marriage, even though there are occasions when only a short time is available and sexual needs are urgent. At such times, "quick sex" can be a loving gift that will be appreciated and rewarded in many ways.

4. **Read some good books.** Men are encouraged to read some good books, also. But it is generally true in our society that women are more inclined to read than are men. Reading keeps one thinking, creative, and trying new things. All of these are healthy for the marriage relationship.

5. **Let go of all inhibitions and participate fully and eagerly.** God intended for the wife to enjoy the sexual relationship, too. Both enjoy it more when both participate eagerly.

6. **Welcome his advances.** In most men, the sex drive is extremely strong. This drive has been given to us by God himself, and it is for the good of both partners in the marriage relationship. It is important for the wife to remember that her husband will feel rejected each time she says "no" to his advances. If she must say "no" (which will be imperative at times), she must learn to say it so her husband feels appreciated instead of rejected.

The sexual relationship between husbands and wives is extremely important. It is the only unique part of a marriage. When two people meet each other's personality needs, sexual intercourse becomes the means of deepening, vitalizing, and enriching one another. We were created by God for this purpose. It allows our one lasting relationship in life to be unique and unlike any other. This permanent, life-long relationship is the only one that can satisfy the deepest hungers for human love.

**7. Become actively involved in the process leading up to the sexual encounter.** A husband's positive feelings about his own sexuality depend a lot on his wife's active, playful participation in the prelude to sexual encounter. Besides, her own pleasure is increased when her husband realizes she is engaging in something she enjoys.

**8. Let him know what pleases you.** Wives must not expect their husbands to know automatically what pleases them. Husbands should know that wives are usually repelled by crude behavior and by vulgar, suggestive language. It is also true that what pleases a wife on one occasion will not necessarily please her later. Two people need to communicate moment to moment what is sexually pleasurable. Communication by words, sounds, and gestures builds the climate that is conducive to happy sexual encounter.

**9. Be creative in initiating love-making.** God intended for the wife to enjoy sexual intimacy as much as the husband. Yet, many women hesitate to be the one to start such loving encounters. But the marriage benefits if she feels free to initiate sexual encounter at times. Most men, in fact, are pleased for their wives to initiate such encounters on a regular basis. Such initiation says volumes to him. It says, "I love you. I need you. I want you. I enjoy being with you. I enjoy our intimate encounters."

10. **Reassure him of his manliness.** The husband's manliness is very important to him. This manhood is regularly beaten down by the world. If his working day is usually difficult, it probably means his ego is threatened, and his manhood takes a beating.

The husband's feelings about himself are at a crucial point when he comes home each evening. That's when he especially needs his wife to respond to him in positive terms as "her man."

I remember hearing a man one time who told how his wife responded to him in a way that built his self-esteem. In fact, she did it for a number of years before he realized how much he needed it. It seems that his wife was especially sensitive to his needs on the days he would sit down to pay the family's bills. During the early years of their marriage, it was quite often impossible to pay all the bills at once. So he had to go through the harrowing experience of deciding which bills to pay this month and which bills to postpone. On each of these evenings, he found to his delight that his wife was sexually aggressive.

Many years later he remembered how important this had been to his feeling about himself, his worth, and his manhood. When a man has failed or when he has been challenged severely and the verdict is not yet in, he has a deep need to be accepted fully as a man by those who are closest to him. The wise wife will see that her man knows how much she loves him, how much she adores him, and how happy she is to be his wife.

Sexual encounter for a husband and wife is God's way for them to keep communication lines open, to love each other, and to share intimately and lovingly with each other.

A good sex life between husband and wife is not something that "just happens." It comes from an atmosphere that they have carefully created all day, all week, all month, and all year for many years. The sexual relationship between husband and wife can be what God wants it to be, and all that it can be, only when two people treat each other in loving ways in every aspect of their lives. The sexual relationship then becomes the frequent, spontaneous celebration of a life of sharing — truly a human expression of a divine love.

# Let's Put Things In Order
## – Family Priorities

Chapter 8

Families today live in an exciting, challenging world. Our potential for happiness has never been greater. Yet, the threats to our happiness have never been more dangerous.

Today's families are more mobile than ever before. We can travel to distant exotic places by jet plane, camper, motor home, or family car. Yet, our mobility also enables us to scatter to the four winds, rarely seeing one another for days at a time.

In a family where each parent has a car and the older children also drive and have cars, home often seems more like a filling station for people, a pit stop on the racetrack of life.

Being at home doesn't guarantee that people will spend time together. Families who spend hours each day watching tv in the same room may not have any idea what is going on in one another's daily concerns.

Watching tv and reading newspapers can provide

us with information about what is going on in the world but cannot inform us about the people who are closest to us.

Even the telephone is proving a mixed blessing, at best, to more and more of us. We enjoy the steps it saves and the access it gives us to others. But the telephone also gives others access to us. It can interrupt a relaxing meal together, pulling one member of the family away from the others for several minutes. Usually the calls are not all that urgent, but rare is the person who makes a habit of deferring phone calls until after dinner.

How many times have we been interrupted in the middle of an important husband-wife discussion or an important time between parent and child by a telephone call that wasn't that important at all! Yet, the moment it interrupted can never be recalled.

All these achievements are marvelous advances, and we would not want to return to that time when none of them were available. But unless we learn ways for them to serve us, they will dictate our lives and threaten the stability of our families.

One additional pressure being exerted on families today is the absence of both father and mother from the family because both engage in full-time employment outside the home. We are thankful that it is possible for men and women to work in reasonable comfort and in activities that are meaningful and satisfying. But we have lost many of the ties that used to bind families together in earlier times.

## Time Together

Back in the days when most people lived on the farm, father and son worked together all day in the field. Mother and daughter worked together all day around the house. A boy learned about farming, but more importantly, he learned about life. While they worked together, he learned about values, faith, and commitment from his dad.

A girl learned about a woman's role in society from her mother. She learned not only how to work, but also drank in the spirit of her mother. She learned about people, about relating, and about spiritual concerns.

When does the modern family find time to spend together like that? How does a boy find out what it means to be a man? When does he find out who his father really is and what he is committed to as a person?

When does a girl spend extended time with her mother finding out about being a woman in today's world? How does her mother communicate to her about life and the things that are really important?

I believe that many families are suffering because both parents are gone "earning a living." We need to recognize the threat, as well as the advantages.

There is a desperate need for families to spend time together. But we live in a hectic world which makes that very difficult. How does a family *make* time to be together?

The first step toward finding an answer to this very searching question would seem to demand some sort of system of priorities. We need a standard to help us measure the importance of each of our many activities. We need some sort of ideal which reflects our basic commitments. We cannot do everything; we must make choices. People without such standards tend to sacrifice what is valuable and end up victims of circumstance.

## GOD — The First Priority

As a Christian, my first priority surely must be the maintaining of a rich, personal, vital relationship with the Almighty. Without that, I have nothing of real value to share with others and no valid base for my own life.

The form which this priority takes will be a very personal thing, but it would seem obvious that this concern must express itself in some kind of daily study of the Bible and communion with the Father in prayer. This "quiet time" with God each day provides the center of the Christian's life, without which all the other activities get out of focus.

We must understand that this priority does not include "work for God." We are not talking about that yet. We are talking here about the feeding of one's own spirit and the daily worship which is so very essential to the Christian's growth.

I cannot imagine a Christian — one who is really serious about his commitment — who does not maintain a daily devotional life. How can spiritual life survive without food? How can growth occur without the intake of essentials to that growth?

Every day there should be a time set aside for Bible study and prayer. It should be considered even more essential than food for the physical body. Job said, ". . . I have treasured in my bosom the words of his mouth" (Job 23:12).

## God/HUSBAND-WIFE

For those who are married, the second priority is the relationship between husband and wife. It takes patience to grow a marriage, experience to discover the ever-changing needs of another human being, courage to communicate, and wisdom to really know another person. Yet, this is what marriage is all about.

Those who are unwilling to take the time that is really needed to nurture a marriage should remain single. But for those who choose to marry, significant investment of time, money, energy, and concern in the relationship is absolutely essential.

For example, I believe that every husband and wife should continue to have "dates" with each other every week. These weekly times together may occasionally be rather expensive, but they do not have to be. Husband and wife desperately need to be together just to be together. To talk, to laugh, to enjoy each other — to be "best friends."

Some couples may be thinking, "We can't afford that." It doesn't have to be expensive. Many enjoyable activities are free and available to the creative couple.

Other couples may be thinking, "But we have small children. We can't afford a sitter once a week." Why not find another couple with young children and "trade-out" once a week while each couple has their special time together? It pays big dividends.

Couples also must learn the art of communication. Each one must develop the capacity to listen, as well as to speak. Each one must encourage the other to grow by taking time to share regularly what each is thinking.

It takes imagination to keep a friendship alive. God created marriage to relieve "aloneness." But simply being together does not serve that purpose of a marriage unless the couple learns more and more the blessings of becoming "one flesh."

# God/Husband-Wife/CHILDREN

For those who are parents, their children are their third priority. The Psalmist tells us that children "are a heritage from the Lord" (Ps. 127:3). Some of the Lord's greatest blessings come to us through life with our children.

Parents are blessed when they bring up their children "in the discipline and instruction of the Lord"

(Eph. 6:4). One of the most satisfying ways of investing our time is to do things with children — to listen and share with them. It takes exacting discipline and sacrifice of lesser priorities, but the rewards God has promised to both children and parents are worth it.

When we bring children into the world, we start a soul toward eternity. I remember the first time that thought really sunk into my consciousness. I was in college — taking the course called "The Christian Home." Our teacher was talking about what it meant to become parents and to "start a soul through life toward eternity." A soul that will never die. A soul that will spend eternity either in heaven or in hell. And the parent is responsible for building into those early years experiences that will predispose the child to a desire to serve God and others. That's heavy responsibility.

---

**"If children become the very center of the family, it is hard for parents to let them grow up and develop their own independent identities."**

---

There is temptation on the part of parents to allow the relationship with children to come before the relationship of husband and wife with each other. But they must not allow this to happen. If children become the very center of the family, it is hard for parents to let them grow up and develop their own independent identities. And when the children finally do grow up and grow away, the parents may find little of their own relationship remaining.

On the other hand, if the husband and wife relationship is at the very center of the family, children can enjoy the security of parental love while orbiting the family in ever-widening circles until they are ready to take their place in society alongside their parents as responsible adults. And when this time comes, the husband/wife relationship is not only still intact, it has been growing as the children grew.

This may sound to some as though I am recommending a course of action which would actually mean neglecting the children in favor of selfish pleasure for the parents. Not at all. Parents must be very careful not to be gone from their children too much. There are special times when children will need attention — when parents simply must not be gone from them.

But such is the case with every basic priority. There are "emergency" situations when other priorities must be suspended for the moment in order that the emergency may be taken care of. Such was the case in the Bible with the man who had been beaten, robbed, and left half-dead (Luke 10:30). No matter where the priest and the Levite were going, they should have stopped and rendered aid. Their other priorities should have been temporarily suspended in order that a matter of great importance might be taken care of.

And so it is with children. Small children are a "walking emergency." They need close and almost constant supervision. But that fact does not change the basic priority — the relationship between husband and wife comes before the relationship between parent and child.

## God/Husband - Wife/Children/ VOCATION

The fourth priority for us as Christians is our means of livelihood. If we give our word in regard to the means by which we make a living, we should by all means be true to that word. If we work for another, we should live up to the basic demands of the job. Integrity demands this. If we are self-employed, we may have greater flexibility. But when we agree to do something, we should let nothing short of an emergency keep us from fulfilling that commitment.

### God/Husband - Wife/Children/Vocation/ SERVICE

As the circle of our concern broadens, we must be ready for ministry everywhere we go. If we belong to Christ, we must be about our Father's business. Caring for the sick, the downtrodden, and the bereaved will be part of our walk with God. Our lives must reflect the same concern that our Lord's life reflected as "He went about doing good."

But if the central concern of the Father was "to seek and save that which was lost," this concern must have a very special place in the life of the Christian. With all the other commitments of our lives, we must not neglect this one. We cannot neglect it and be true to the Lord.

---

**"Appropriate priorities help us to reflect the things we value the most."**

---

Appropriate priorities help us to reflect the things we value the most. They do not solve all the problems, but they give us something to use as a measuring device when less important things seem to be crowding out things of greater importance.

Every family feels that pressure — too many things to be done and not enough time to do them all.

It is sobering to read the words of Joshua 24:15, ". . . as for me and my house, we will serve the Lord," and then to realize that after such great resolve, ". . . there arose another generation after

131

them, who did not know the Lord or work which he had done for Israel" (Judg. 2:10).

One generation had already been lost in the wilderness. God had called his people back to him and back to their great responsibilities as families in the words of Deuteronomy 6:4-9:

> Hear, O Israel: The LORD our God is one LORD; and you shall love the LORD your God with all your heart, and with all your soul, and with all your might. And these words which I command you this day shall be upon your heart; and you shall teach them diligently to your children, and shall talk of them when you sit in your house, and when you walk by the way, and when you lie down, and when you rise. And you shall bind them as a sign upon your hand, and they shall be as frontlets between your eyes. And you shall write them on the doorposts of your house and on your gates.

Such explicit instructions indicated exactly what had gone wrong and how the difficulties were to be solved.

One can almost feel the emotion as Moses spoke the words, "You must love the Lord your God . . . ." Jesus would say some fifteen hundred years later: "This is the great and first commandment" (Matt. 22:37, 38). None of us are ready to tell another about God until there is first a deep love in our own hearts.

"And these words which I command you this day shall be upon your heart" (vs. 6). The next step is to truly treasure the word of God, to hunger and thirst for it, to feast regularly upon it, and to saturate one's inner life with that word.

## Parents as Models

The first responsibility of parents is to "model" the

role of a devoted servant of God for their children. If the model is faulty, the message will be garbled and confused, no matter how clear the words.

"And you shall teach them diligently to your children . . ." (vs.7). Parents cannot avoid their responsibilities as teachers. *They will teach.* But their teaching will be inadequate without *words.* Even with a powerful example, many concepts will be unclear unless they are explained carefully to a growing child.

". . . You shall talk of them when you sit in your house . . . " (vs. 7). Is that meal time? Surely this would be one such time that could be used to great advantage.

". . . And when you walk by the way . . ." (vs. 7). Families often walked long distances together in the ancient world, and such occasions allowed extended time for parents to carry on lengthy conversations about important subjects. Perhaps a parallel in our day would be those times when families travel together. Parents need some creativity and ingenuity to really use such time wisely, for such periods offer rare opportunities for teaching.

". . . And when you lie down . . ." (vs. 7). That's bedtime. There is a special "openness" for a child at bedtime. Everyone enjoys attention. A parent who is genuinely interested in keeping up with the interests of his child will find "teachable moments" in abundance at such times in a growing child's life.

". . . And when you rise up . . ." (vs. 7). This is breakfast time. I know families that have a "scripture-for-the-day" at the breakfast table. Such passages, carefully selected, can be a powerful influence in each person's day as the members of a family scatter to be "God's person" in a challenging world.

The "sign upon the hand," "frontlets between the

eyes," and "writing on the doorposts of your house and on your gates" (vss. 8, 9), may indicate, for the modern home, signs of the family's commitment. Keep Bibles, tracts, commentaries, religious periodicals, and the like in conspicious places around the house.

---

## "Someone must plan specifically in order that the really good things may happen in the life of a family."

---

What unspeakable joy there is in seeing a family where each member, at his own rate, is growing in his commitment and service to God. Nothing is more important. The highest priority for Christian families is the time they spend together. The only thing more important, as we pointed out above, is the believer's own spiritual commitments. Nothing is more effective in edging out evil influences. Someone must be paying attention, not just drifting along. Someone must take time to investigate the influences being brought to bear on family members. Someone must plan specifically in order that the really good things may happen in the life of a family. We must "take charge," aggressively take charge like a mother lion with her cubs. We must provide for the needs of our families with that kind of *life-risking* dedication. We must protect family members from destructive forces with that same kind of enthusiasm and commitment.

We live in an exciting, challenging world. There has never been a time like this time. The potential is staggering. But with every possibility there is an accompanying threat.

What kind of life shall my family live? That depends. It depends on the values we hold, on the sacri-

134

fices we are willing to make, on the family goals that we are really willing to work on to make happen, and on our willingness to allow God to direct and empower.

If our values and goals grow out of our commitment to him, the possibilities for family life in these exciting times are unlimited.

There is in every family a potential family waiting to be born. We catch occasional glimpses of it, but it is a frightening vision to many. "It would cost too much" they think, so they walk sadly away.

# Lord, Give Me Wisdom
## – Parenting Children

### Chapter 9

For many years, Sam Davis Tatum was judge of the juvenile court in Davidson County (Nashville), Tennessee. The emotional pressure of his work was very heavy as he dealt constantly with families undergoing extremely difficult times.

The judge used to tell a story about an experience he had which reminded him of the importance of the family unit. He was fishing one day in a river near Nashville. As he waded up the river, casting as he went, his boot struck a small sandbar. Suddenly, half a dozen or so very small turtles appeared on top of the water, swimming for all they were worth.

The judge reflected: Here were small turtles that had never seen their parents. A mother turtle had laid her eggs in the warm sand of a river bank and had left them there as she went on with her life.

In time, by the providence of God, the little turtles were born, equipped from birth to take care of themselves in the world. They never saw their mother and father nor never knew they had or needed such. They were totally unaware that there was any other way to live.

The judge thought, "How different it is for human families." In his mind he pictured a human family, waiting for a baby to be born. Suddenly, lights go on in the middle of the night. An engine races as father takes mother to the hospital to await that moment when a new member will be born into this family. As lights appear in distant cities, phone calls announce the news. Two other families — the grandparents — pack their bags and begin a journey to participate in one of the most important events in the world — the arrival of a new member of a family.

Unlike the newborn in the animal world, the human newborn needs close attention, supervision, and care, not just for a few months but for many years. The infant will not be ready to be "out on his own" for eighteen to twenty years. What a tremendous difference between the animal and the human families! Yet, we realize that this is part of the order that God has created. The differences will determine the quality of life and destiny.

Being a parent is a fantastic challenge. The God-given potentials of any child are the most intriguing and exciting in all creation. The capacity for good or bad, for ministry and service or destruction, are all there, wrapped up in the frail body of a new life.

Four great principles for parent-child relationships seem to emerge from scripture.

## First Principle: Leadership

The first of these is the principle of leadership. Children's first step in learning about leadership is to ". . . obey your parents in the Lord, for this is right" (Eph. 6:1). Developing a capacity for leadership begins in the home when a child is very small or it probably will never be part of that person's personality. It grows best when the one in authority, the parent, reflects a deep respect for the child. The parent who has a healthy respect for the rights and needs of the child will be in the best position to receive respect in return. Appreciation for the skills of leadership will develop naturally as the child's world expands to include becoming a leader in the church, the school, the community, and the world at large.

The parent takes the leadership role for the growing child until he is ready to accept full responsibility for himself. When the child is very young, close supervision is absolutely essential. A "childproof" environment — one with breakables, poisons, and valuables out of reach — must exist to protect the child from danger until he is old enough to recognize and respond appropriately to each danger.

As the child's world expands, the supervision can more and more take the form of "rules" that the child is to use as guidelines for his behavior. The next instruction in Ephesians 6 says, "Honor your father and your mother. . ." (vs. 2). This instruction applies appropriately to the child as he ventures out into the world—for brief periods only at first—away from his parents. He is to begin to govern his own behavior. And this is to be done in such a way as to reflect honor upon his parents.

## Second Principle: Instruction

The next principle for parents is that of *teaching* or *instruction*. Parents are responsible for teaching their children about the world, about relationships, about right and wrong, and about all the important aspects of daily living. It is difficult for parents to realize that a child has to learn even such simple things as: paper tears, glass breaks, fire burns, flowers take time to grow, and a myriad of other things.

Broken glass or milk and food on the floor look horrible to an adult, but they may look "beautiful" to a child. Drapes that have been cut by scissors and a wall marked with crayon horrify an adult who has spent hundreds of dollars getting a room to look just this way, but a child does not automatically know the difference, which is so obvious to the parent. All of this must be learned. And the learning process is often very frustrating to both the teacher and the learner.

As the child grows and begins to relate to other people, special rules of social behavior must be learned. I remember some of the experiences we went through as a family as our children were coming through those very early years. One of the things we did for several years was to have "family night."

This special night for our family to be together served a number of functions — several of which we were probably not aware of. But one of the specific goals of these evenings was to teach our children table manners.

We are a family that doesn't believe one has to use his *very best* manners all the time. We usually eat our meals in a very relaxed atmosphere. We reach for things that are "reasonably close" rather than interrupt another person's meal. We also allow the unused hand (and its elbow) to be in other places than the lap.

But we felt a deep need to teach our children appropriate manners for their own sense of comfort and security when they were around those other than members of their own family. The plan we developed was to have a special meal together as a family every Friday night. For this meal, the family dining room was used. We also used the best dishes and silverware (it was stainless steel).

All members of the family dressed up a bit for this occasion, and all helped set the table (valuable training in "where everything goes"). During the meal, children were instructed and trained in the use of proper manners (which fork to use when and for what; "Pass the peas, please"; hand in the lap; etc.).

It was a delightful experience for the family. We all looked forward to it, and it allowed us to teach our children some very important things.

---

## "We discovered that the children delighted in learning to quote scripture when father or mother made a game of learning."

---

Another part of our teaching responsibility was biblical instruction. Ephesians 6:4 instructs, ". . . bring them up in the discipline and instruction of the Lord." Deuteronomy 6:6, 7 says, ". . . these words . . . teach them *diligently* to your children. . . ." How do parents go about this?

The method we chose was a devotional with our children each night at bedtime. We started these when our first baby was about a year old, and each additional child was added to the circle as he was able to enjoy the attention and participate in a parent's lap.

We all sat in a circle on the floor, usually in the den, for the experiences. At first the periods were very brief. We would sing the little hand-action songs so familiar to the children in their Vacation Bible School classes. We would have a very brief prayer together. Then, off to bed for the children.

As the children got a little older, we would let each

one suggest a song for the family to sing. Following the singing, we would quote favorite scriptures.

We discovered that the children delighted in learning to quote scripture when father or mother made a game of learning. I would say to the child, "Say this with me four times: 'For God so loved the world.' " Each time I would point at the child, first with one finger, then two, and so forth until we had said this four times. Then, we would do this again with the next short phrase "that he gave his only begotten son. . . ." When that one had been repeated four times, we would go to the next until each part of the verse had been repeated four times.

Over a period of several years, we were amazed at how many verses our small children learned to quote and what an enjoyable experience they thought it had been to have that kind of parental and family attention.

During those years, we always ended our devotionals with a chain prayer, each member of the family participating as he/she voiced his/her concerns and thanksgiving to the Father. We found that it was very helpful to preface the period of prayer with a time of talking about "what happened today that you want to talk to God about." This helped to keep them from saying the same prayers over and over again.

Of course, there were "teachable moments," in addition to these structured times; but those years quickly passed and the form of the instruction had to "change with the times."

## Third Principle: Transferring Responsibility

A third principle of parenting that is very crucial is transfer of responsibility. One of the great goals of every Christian parent is to train up a responsible human being. We want our children, when they are grown, to have a deep sense of responsiblity, duty, and discipline. If our children grow up to accomplish great good in their own lives and in the lives of others, we have realized a very important ingredient in successful parenting.

But responsibility, like so many other things, begins best at an early age. A good rule of thumb is: never do for a child what he can do for himself. There will be times, especially early in the child's life, when that rule must be broken in the interest of time, family schedule, or maybe in the interest of "love." But it is, nevertheless, a pretty good rule.

As soon as a child can begin to dress himself and tie his own shoes, he should be *encouraged to do so*. The same goes for picking up toys and putting them in their proper place, putting away clothes, making the bed, and cleaning the room.

---

## *"Love establishes limits for parental authority."*

---

The older child should handle part of the family chores, such as taking out trash, clearing away the table, dusting, or vacuuming. These responsibilities can actually give a growing child a deep sense of "belonging" if the parents display a good attitude.

The full transfer of responsibility should be a gradual thing and started very early. The time will come when parents must "turn loose" and untie the apron strings. But the child who has not been properly prepared is not ready. For one, who has not been allowed to grow gradually in responsibility, to have full responsibility may be disastrous. These early years and the gradual increase of responsibility are crucial considerations for a foundation being laid for future responsible action as an adolescent and as an adult.

The days quickly come when the adolescent is more and more "out on his own." By driver's license age, he/she must more and more be trusted away from adult supervision. The basis for a successful experience at these points is laid during the early years of training in responsibility.

## Fourth Principle: Love for the Child

The fourth principle of parenting is that of love. Love for the child must permeate and govern every contact with the child. Love means that we are aware of the importance of an individual, realizing a child is due every courtesy and consideration that other human beings are due. Love means that we are constantly aware of a child's needs as an individual and that we constantly keep at the heart of our relationship his greatest good as a person.

Love for the child must be the guiding principle in establishing guidelines for the first three principles that we have talked about. Love establishes limits for parental authority. That authority must not be rough and harsh. Fathers are commanded, ". . . do not provoke your children to anger. . ." (Eph. 6:4). Authority is essential for the child's welfare, but it must be exercised gently, with care and consideration.

Love suggests the guidelines for parental instruction: "What does my child need to know and understand in order to be a productive and happy person, both today and in the future?"

Love is the basis for the transfer of responsibility to the growing child. Not just "What can my child do for me that would take part of my heavy work load away?" but "What responsibilities can my child assume that will be good not only for the rest of the

143

family but, even more important, that will increase my child's sense of belonging today and equip him/her to live a fully responsible and productive life in the future?"

Love is the greatest need of every human being. All other needs are tributaries to this one. I believe this is central to the divine design for the family. This is why God put us together in this unique way.

God made the newborn child to need love so desperately that he cannot live the first year of his life without it. Many illustrations of this fact are on record. One stands out in my mind that makes the point.

Near the turn of this century a unique and widespread phenomenon took place. In major cities in various parts of the world, people began to leave newborn babies on the doorsteps of others whom they hoped would keep and raise them. This in itself was not something new, but the numbers of such occurrences was voluminous. So many were being left that demands were made for city governments to make some provisions for taking care of such infants.

As cities responded with institutional care, the flood of infants increased. Such institutions were obviously understaffed, and the frustrations of having to do a job that could not be done right must have been horrible. Staff members decided that the only logical course was to do the best they could with a bad situation. They would do their best to keep the children fed and clean, while working towards more help to take care of other needs.

What they found was that a baby cannot live without "tender love and care." They could feed him a nutritious, well-balanced diet and keep him reasonably clean so that illness would not be likely. Yet, without someone to love him — to hold, talk, and pay attention to him — he could not survive the first year of his life.

God made us this way! He designed human beings for love! And he put us together in families to insure we would be loved.

He designed the man and the woman for "togetherness" and love. In the basic design of the marriage relationship, God provided for children to be born. It is in the most intimate, loving expression of their "oneness" that a child is conceived. And into the midst of that oneness, permeated by the love of two people for each other, God designed that a child shall be born. That child is the unique product of their love. By divine design, this is the likeliest environment for the healthy development of a human being.

---

## "... the father and mother ... need to love each other in ways that the children can see."

---

It is also important to realize that God arranged it so that a child cannot get here without both a father and a mother. Both the female ovum and the male sperm are essential to new life. We can separate the two, but it is the divine design that every child have the continuing influence in his life of both a mother and a father who love each other and the child.

Dr. John White, a noted Canadian psychiatrist with a strong biblical thrust to his work, reminds us that the love of a father and mother for each other is even more important in the child's development than the love that either shows the child.[1]

You have seen the sign that says, "The greatest thing I can do for my children is to love their mother." That's basic — that the father and mother love each other. And they need to love each other in ways that the children can *see*. That love between parents provides the backdrop for the love that the child experiences.

It is extremely important for parents to learn to extend their love in ways that the child actually perceives as "love." Many parents who really love their children sometimes show it in ways that only the parents can see, rather than in ways that come through to the child. The child perceives parental love in many ways, but several are especially important.

**Time.** The parent who has no time for the child cannot really communicate love for that child, regardless of how real the love may be. Many parents try to substitute gifts for time, but gifts are an inadequate expression of love. What the child wants is not the parent's gifts but the parent's *time*.

**Attention.** How many times during these early years does a child say, "See my new dress?" or "See what I made in school." or "Daddy, watch." Parental attention is extremely important to the child's self-concept. Attention says, "You are important. I love you."

**Listening.** One of the basic needs of every human being is the need to be important. And one of the best ways to show another's importance is to listen — really *listen*. Through listening, parents not only find out what's going on in the child's life, but also lay the groundwork for the child to listen to them. A child who is not listened to will not listen.

**Training.** Basic training for the everyday tasks of life are essential to healthy growth. Such basic tasks as bathing, washing one's hands, brushing teeth, setting the table, and sweeping the floor must be learned. And they are best learned by watching an experienced, respected, loving "helper."

**Doing things with the child that the child wants to do.** The parent who reads, plays, walks, and talks with the child is forming a basic relationship with that growing human being that says, "I love you."

**Encouragement.** The apostle Paul said, ". . .like a father with his children, we exhorted each one of you and encouraged you . . ." (1 Thess. 2:11). Many parents find themselves drifting into the habit of being primarily negative with their children. But best results are achieved by the positive, encouraging things that we say to them.

Someone has said, "If we would find more things in our children to commend, there would be fewer things to criticize."

Our children need our encouragement. As we focus on their assets and strengths, rather than on their weaknesses and failures, we help them build a good self-concept. This means recognizing improvement and effort as well as accomplishment. It means expecting something really special from our children and encouraging them as they respond to those expectations.

## Children Learn What They Live

If a child lives with criticism, he learns to condemn.

If a child lives with hostility, he learns to fight.

If a child lives with fear, he learns to be apprehensive.

If a child lives with pity, he learns to feel sorry for himself.

If a child lives with jealousy, he learns to feel guilty.

If a child lives with encouragement, he learns to be confident.

If a child lives with tolerance, he learns to be patient.

147

If a child lives with praise, he learns to be appreciative.

If a child lives with acceptance, he learns to love.

If a child lives with approval, he learns to like himself.

If a child lives with recognition, he learns it is good to have a goal.

If a child lives with fairness, he learns what justice is.

If a child lives with honesty, he learns what truth is.

If a child lives with security, he learns to have faith in himself and those about him.

If a child lives with friendliness, he learns the world is a nice place in which to live.

— Author unknown.

Each family must work out the patterns of their own relationships. No two families will be alike. We would commend to your family, however, the following ten guidelines for parents as children grow through the first twelve years of life. These have been extremely helpful to us.

## Guidelines For Rearing Children

1. Remember that every child needs two Christian parents.
2. Help your child learn about limits.
3. Help your child learn that every action has consequences, some happy and some disappointing.
4. Allow each child to be an individual, and never compare him with others.
5. Never promise or threaten that which you do not intend to carry out.
6. Offer authentic manifestations of love, not just superficial ones.

7. Teach your child basic principles of leadership.
8. Do not condone the faults of your children through a misguided sense of loyalty.
9. Be careful always to be a good example.
10. Teach your children that God loves them and that they can have a close relationship with him.

---

[1]John White, *Eros Defiled* (Downers Grove: Inter-Varsity Press, 1977).

# Lord, Give Me Understanding
## –Parenting Adolescents

Chapter 10

For some people, the teen years are extremely difficult — passing with agonizing, turtle-like slowness. But for parents, entrusted with the task of helping children become adults, the time passes all too quickly.

During a child's first twelve years, almost all the authority and responsibility belong to the parent. With the onset of puberty some dramatic changes take place in the child's life. These changes make a tremendous impact on every aspect of the child's existence. The child's physical body has been rather easily controlled by adults who were so much larger and more powerful. Now, suddenly, the child begins to develop the body of an adult. As the adult body develops, the adolescent becomes increasingly difficult to control from the outside.

The teenager thinks, "I am almost an adult now. Why shouldn't I have more 'say' in my life? Why shouldn't I be allowed more adult privileges? Why should someone else always tell me what to do?"

And the parent may think, "Help, my child is slipping away from me." In a few years the adolescent will graduate from high school. When graduation comes, important changes will affect the lives of most adolescents. They normally move on to college or to a job. In either case, they move away from home and from parental supervision.

## Growing Up and Away

The struggle of these adolescent years is small for some but very large for others. The Bible gives strong adolescent examples, such as Abel, Daniel, David, Miriam, Esther, and Mary. But we also recall the struggles and the sins of young people like Cain, Esau, Absalom, Delilah, and Salome.

In some ways, the link between parents and their teenagers acts like a rubber band. The adolescent years demand a certain "growing up" and "growing away." Growing independence is absolutely essential during these years if normal development is to take place.

If the rate of growing independence is agreed upon by both parent and child, the tension on the rubber band is minimal. The rubber band has certain elasticity and can stand some "strain" without difficulty. But if the teenager wants too much independence too soon, or if parents are reluctant to turn over the control to the teenager as rapidly as the teenager would like, the tension can become almost unbearable.

The goal is "total independence by eighteen." The approach is "gradual transfer of responsibility." Ideally, a parent will try to move from a position of ultimate control when a child is about twelve years of age. By the time the teenager is about eighteen, the parent will have shifted to the role of a consultant or counselor.

The path toward the goal of independence may be very rocky; but it is far better to have a goal than to let events happen without one. And it is also good to communicate the ideal with our children. We can let them know that we're aware they are growing up and will soon be out on their own. We don't need to hesitate telling a child, "We don't believe you are quite ready for that yet. Let's start working for the time when you'll be ready." Sometimes a "no" is more tolerable if it is a "later."

## Building Good Families

Keeping the lines of communication open between teenagers and parents during this time takes some very special planning. I remember an experience that I had several years ago which brought this fact home to me in a very powerful way.

A noted speech professor and personal friend of mine visited our campus for a speaking engagement. We were to eat the evening meal together in the A.C.U. cafeteria, and as we sat down to eat, he said rather casually to me, "Carl, what are you and Smitty doing to keep the lines of communication open with your children?" As we ate our meal, I began to tell him about some of the things we were doing as a family. Then, I asked him, "What are you and your wife doing to keep the lines of communication open with your kids?" He began to tell me about their concerns for their family.

For years he and his wife had been "family watchers." They had been on the look-out for families who seemed to be doing an especially good job. They watched for family closeness, healthy parent-child relationship, and responsible children, both with and apart from their parents. When they discovered such a family, they would make a special opportunity to be with them and to ask the question, "What have you done to keep the lines of communication open with your children? Tell us about your family." The professor said they had heard many good ideas over the years, as one would imagine. But in all of the families, what was said boiled down to these four characteristics:

**Open affection.** All of the families expressed love for one another openly and spontaneously. They engaged in a lot of hugging and gentle touching. Proverb 27:5 says, "Better is open rebuke than hidden love." Many people have difficulty expressing their feelings, especially appreciation and love. So many couples who cannot naturally hug and touch tenderly, live with tension and sullenness, and later, as parents, they do not touch and hug their children.

**Mutual Support.** These families took an interest in the activities of each member. If one member was involved in a drama production or an athletic event, the entire family would attend the event together. Each member of the family would support the participating member in appropriate ways: applause, a smile, a pat on the back, and/or a word of commendation.

How many thrilling occasions arise for families to watch each member grow! Yet, how many parents are "too busy" to be involved with their children — missing that which they will later regret.

**Rituals.** Each family member often participated in "family rituals" together. Some obvious rituals were: meals eaten together, family prayer at meal time, going to church together, and family devotionals. Less frequent activities, which depended on family preference, were: family vacations, backpacking, camping, fishing, and hiking. Still other rituals included a certain group of family members:

153

a mother-daughter meal out, a father-son workout at a health club, a father-daughter movie, or a mother-son tennis match.

Endless opportunities exist for such rituals. The key is that they allow family members to be together doing something that they enjoy. Such experiences build deep, strong family ties and provide a solid foundation for the building of a life.

Such rituals can be found in the Bible. An especially important one came during Passover when the youngest child would ask, "Father, what do these things mean?" Regardless of how many times the child had heard it, the father told the story once more. A similar ritual was established when the children of Israel crossed the Jordan and set up the twelve stones in Gilgal. Joshua told the people, "When your children ask their fathers in time to come, 'What do these stones mean?' then you shall let your children know 'Israel passed over this Jordan on dry ground' " (Joshua 4:21, 22).

**Decisive living.** Strong family ties did not leap into existence by themselves; they were built *on purpose*. The father and mother sat down regularly to *plan*, asking questions, such as: What are we currently missing in the life of our family that would enrich us? What are we missing that we will later look back and regret? Is there too much absence of either father or mother from the family, which works against the family's good? Are we doing some things that we can curtail in order to have more time together?

Decisive living means that families take charge of their lives and make things happen. Too many families drift along and are subject to whatever happens — good, bad, or indifferent. If we want to increase the amount of good that happens in our family, we need to find out how to *make it happen*!

## Patterns For Strong Families

The professor's experiences took place several years ago, but they closely parallel the results of some recent studies in Oklahoma. A research team from Oklahoma State University made an in-depth study of ninety-nine strong, Oklahoma families in an attempt to find out what made these families strong. Five patterns from these strong families began to emerge very early in the study:

1. Members of these families expressed appreciation to each other very often.
2. They spent a lot of time together. As a matter of fact, they intentionally cut down on the number of outside activities and involvements in order to minimize fragmentation of their family life.
3. They worked hard at keeping lines of communication open and keeping their communication as positive as possible.
4. These strong families were devout. They were active in a church as a family, and beyond that, they regularly read the Bible and prayed together. But most importantly, they had a constant sense that God cares and is involved in the daily processes of their lives.
5. They were committed to the family, to spending time together and to making each other happy.[1]

## Affirming Each Other

One of the things our own family has tried with good results is that near the conclusion of the evening meal, one family member is asked, "What do you see as your strongest point as a person?" After that person has thought about it for a moment and has answered the question, each of the other family members offers additional strong qualities that he sees in that person. Each family member in turn is asked to respond to the same question and all of the others offer additional strong qualities. In this way, family members have an opportunity to "affirm" each other verbally.

Everybody thrives on this kind of affirmation — even parents. It is good for children to be affirmed by each other, as well as by their parents, and good for young and old alike to experience affirming others. Ultimately, it is good training for the development of future relationships.

## Keeping Communication Lines Open

I know one father who took advantage of a special opportunity to be with his teenage daughter, which reaped positive results. The daughter was fighting the tendency to put on weight and decided she needed to jog a couple of miles every day. Her schedule was such that it was difficult to find the time after school or at night, so she decided on 6:00 A.M. It was dangerous for her to be out alone, so her father volunteered to jog with her every morning.

For the next two years, they jogged together; and thus, father and daughter became very close. They found time to discuss many subjects, and communication lines stayed open to a higher degree because of their joint activity. They now know each other to an extent that would not have been likely without the jogging, and the memories they share will strengthen their relationship for years to come.

That same father created a similar experience with his fifteen-year-old son. The son was not interested in jogging but was very interested in weightlifting and bodybuilding. Three days a week the two visited a health club, each having his own routine and goal. Coming home after their workout, they would occasionally eat a meal together (breakfast after an early-morning workout was especially delightful). The father did not press the conversation, nor did he use the time to "preach" or "get in his licks." He would follow any conversation into areas he knew his son was interested in and comfortable with. Just the chance to be together, doing something the son enjoyed, allowed their relationship to grow, and it kept their lines of communication open through some otherwise difficult times.

A mother I know shared a health club experience with her daughter. The daughter was deeply concerned about her figure and its development. The mother agreed to go with her to the health club five times a week for several months. The experience was great for their relationship.

## Modeling A Life-style

Good parents are not those who have best mastered the "techniques." Many parents believe that all they have to do is learn a few techniques and "presto" they are good parents. Good parents are basically good people. Our children learn far more from what we do than from what we say. All the family devotionals in the world will not help a child's faith grow if his parents are not themselves committed to the Lord.

Parenting grows out of a life-style. The most effective parents are, in general terms, good people with a "feel" for good values and good human relationships. But, given those basic ingredients, it also helps to develop certain habits that enhance, rather than diminish, the growing adolescent's self-image.

## Developing Listening Skills

One such habit is active listening. It is amazing to observe what happens in our relationships with others — including our own children — when we develop the skill of listening to what they are saying.

157

There is no better way to fill another person's need for respect than by being a good listener.

But learning to listen to an adolescent is not always that easy. Many adolescents go through what some have called the "cave years." From about fourteen to seventeen they draw inside themselves, become silent, and are reluctant to communicate. If parents can learn to communicate that they are "interested" but not "nosy," it is still possible to keep lines of communication open even during those difficult years.

One friend of mine tells the story of the day his daughter came storming through the house and slamming doors after school saying, "This has been a horrible day. Everything has gone wrong, and I don't want to talk about it!" She went to her room and slammed the door.

Both parents sat stunned for a little while. Then, they decided that the best way to handle it was to leave her alone for the time being. When supper was ready, the father tapped quietly on the door of the daughter's room and said, "Supper is ready. Would you like something to eat?" The daughter had had time to cool down and was ready to become sociable again. During the course of the meal, her father said, "We would like to hear about your day and what went wrong, but we are willing to wait until you are ready to talk about it." With that kind of non-demanding invitation to share, the daughter opened up and told them about her day.

Another family has "something interesting happened to me today" time as part of their evening mealtime together. Each member shares an experience from the day with the others. It doesn't always have to be a good experience; it may be a bad one. Thus, it allows family members an insight into each other's life.

# Rules and Agreements

As graduation from high school approaches, several very crucial issues will face parents and teenagers.

One is the driver's license. This is such an important time in the adolescent's life. He sees all kinds of possibilities; but mostly, he sees independence — spelled with a capital "I."

We have told our children, "You can begin dating when you are sixteen." That may sound terribly "old-fogeyish" to many parents, but to us it seems to make good sense. We make a few exceptions to that rule before they are sixteen — banquets and other special occasions. But the exceptions must be talked out and negotiated.

What about the car and its use by the teenagers who have driver's licenses? We decided that there needed to be some clearly understood guidelines. We found that some other parents had developed driving agreements, so we borrowed some of their ideas, added some of our own, and came up with the following:

### Preliminary Driving Agreement

1. If I want to go somewhere for myself, my homework must be completed thoroughly.
2. Before using either car, I will ask either my mom or dad if I can use the car and explain the purpose.
3. I will not allow anyone else to drive the car under any circumstances.
4. I will not give rides to hitchhikers under any conditions.
5. I will not carry more than five passengers in the car at any time.
6. During the first six months of driving with

159

my own driver's license, the radio will not be used while driving.

7. If I have to pay a fine for a traffic violation, driving privileges will be suspended for one month.
8. If I have to pay a second fine for a traffic violation within 12 months after the first, driving privileges will be suspended for six months.
9. I will either wash the car or have it done once every three weeks.
10. I will pay half of the increase of the insurance costs and, in case of an accident, I will assume half of the deductible cost.

(Adapted from a similar work by
Norman Wright.)

What about teenagers having their own cars? Some parents will scream "no way"; others will buy cars for their teenagers. Our approach has been to tell our children well before they reach sixteen, "When you get your driver's license, we will pay half the cost if you want to buy your own car." None of ours have taken us up on that yet. The car they could afford, even with their parents' half, they would not have. But the possibility of being able and trusted to buy their own car has been good for their self-confidence.

Another part of growing up is learning to handle money. We have given our children weekly allowances from earliest childhood. We have given them money for the contribution at church as a special, designated part of that allowance.

As our teenagers reached their sophomore year in high school, we told them, "Next year we want you to begin handling your own finances. We will work with you and help you make decisions when you want us to, but we want you to work out a budget that you think will fit your needs. In anticipation of that, this year you will need to keep careful records of everything you spend — both what you spend on yourself and what we spend on you. We will use those records to help us work out a budget for you when the time comes."

---

**"A little financial responsibility sends a lot of nonverbal signals to teenagers that they need to hear: 'We love you.'"**

---

The anticipation of handling their own financial affairs is both exciting and sobering to a teenager. The experience of working out a budget together is good for the parent-teen relationship. For most teenagers, the actual experience of having their own checking and savings account produces splendid growth in responsibility, even though supervision is needed at first. A little financial responsibility sends a lot of nonverbal signals to teenagers that they need to hear: "We love you. We trust you. We want you to grow up. We want to help you as you learn to accept more and more responsibility for your own life."[2]

We have also found this training to be excellent background for the college years when teenagers must handle their financial affairs without close adult supervision.

Then, there is the matter of rules. When do parents stop making rules for their offspring? The most common answer has been, "When they move out of the parental home and are no longer being supported by their parents." Technically, that answer is correct, but there is surely a better way. If our theory is correct, responsibility for one's choices and behavior needs to be turned over to the person gradually.

So it follows that each year fewer and fewer rules should be imposed by parents on their teenagers until they leave home permanently.

Our approach has been to set early goals and say to each child, "By your senior year in high school, we would like for you to be making all your own rules." That sounds, on the surface, like complete freedom; but they know it is not. Hopefully, the teenager has begun to internalize the standards the family lives by. These standards formed the early base and are still there. But in the day-to-day decisions of life, it is time for the teenager to feel increasing freedom.

## Looking For the Stars

The teen years pass quickly. There may be difficult days for both parents and teenagers, but if parents will approach the experiences of these years with enthusiasm and optimism, they can also be exciting years.

The story is told of a young bride from the East who, during the last war, followed her husband to an army camp on the edge of a desert in California. Living conditions were primitive at best. He had advised against her moving there, but she wanted to be with him.

The only housing they could find was a run-down shack near an Indian village. The heat was unbearable in the daytime, reaching 115 degrees in the shade. The wind blew constantly, spreading dust and sand on everything in the house. The days were long and boring because her only neighbors were the Indians, none of whom spoke English.

When her husband was ordered farther into the desert for two weeks of maneuvers, loneliness and the wretched living conditions got the best of her. She wrote to her mother that she was coming home — she just couldn't take it any more. In a short time, she received a reply that included these two lines:

Two men looked out from prison bars,
One saw mud, the other saw stars.

She read the lines over and over and began to feel ashamed of herself. She didn't really want to leave her husband. "All right!" she said to herself. She would look for the stars.

In the days that followed, she set out to make friends with the Indians. She asked them to teach her weaving and pottery. At first, they were distant; but as soon as they sensed that her interest was genuine, they returned her friendship. She became fascinated with their culture, history — everything about them.

She began to study the desert as well; and soon it, too, changed from a desolate, forbidding place to a marvelous thing of beauty. She had her mother send her books and studied the forms of the cacti, the yuccas, and the Joshua trees. Later, she became such an expert on the area that she wrote a book about it.

The desert didn't change. The Indians didn't change. Simply by changing her own attitude she had transformed a miserable experience into a highly rewarding one.

It doesn't take long for children to grow up. It can be a lot of fun if you approach it determined to make it that way.

---

[1]Reported in *Family Strengths Magazine* (Fall 1976), pp. 6-8.
[2]Charlie W. Shedd, *You Can Be A Great Parent* (Menlo Park: Word Books, 1976).

# What Are We Going To Do?
## – Creative Discipline

Chapter 11

To watch a life unfold — to be directly and intimately involved as a guide to maturity and a supervisor of growth — is what makes being a parent one of the most exciting and rewarding experiences in the world.

Daniel Webster said it this way:

If we work upon marble, it will perish; if we work upon brass, time will efface it; if we rear temples, they will crumble into dust; but if we work upon immortal souls, if we imbue them with principles, with the just fear of the Creator and love of fellowman, we engrave on those tablets something which will brighten all eternity.

We cannot be parents without dreaming dreams. In our arms we hold the future with all its hopes, expectations, and possibilities. What are our dreams for our children?

Admittedly, some parents merely want to relive

their own lives through their children. They want their children to fulfil the longings and hopes that never came true in their lives. As a result, such parents unfairly try to manipulate their children to be little more than extensions of themselves.

Parents who grew up in a happy environment will want to bring up children who have minds of their own. They will try to help the child to grow to maturity as a healthy, responsible, and loving person. Along the way, the process necessarily will include many frustrations, irritations, and failures.

## The Goal of Discipline

The goal of all good discipline is self-discipline. As parents, we want to help our children to develop inner strength and independence to make happy, healthy lives for themselves. We want our children to learn to live their lives without us — in fact, without needing anyone to exert pressure from the outside. We want to help our children develop an inner pressure to do right. We accomplish that by using the principles of good discipline from early infancy until our children are able to "walk alone."

The word *discipline* comes from the same root word as the word *disciple*. We usually think of discipline only in terms of unpleasant experiences, but this is too limited a view. We need to think of discipline in its larger context: instruction, guidance, help, and training. Discipline will surely include some unpleasant experiences, but these cannot be effective unless they are outweighed by pleasant aspects.

Good discipline begins with a loving, accepting environment. It begins when a parent plays, feeds, reads, walks, and talks with the child. Discipline means listening and responding patiently to the

165

child. The child is a learner (disciple). It is only in this kind of environment that the unpleasant experiences of discipline can really have their desired impact. The child must feel safe within well-defined limits. The Bible prepares us to accept and deal with the less pleasant experiences. The Wise Man said, "Folly is bound up in the heart of a child, but the rod of discipline drives it far from him" (Prov. 22:15). And again, "Do not withhold discipline from a child; if you beat him with a rod, he will not die . . . you will save his soul from Sheol" (Prov. 23:13, 14).

Small children do not yet have the maturity, the self-discipline, nor even the knowledge to do the right thing. If children do not *know*, they need information and instruction. Once children know, they need supervision that puts appropriate pressure on them to act in accordance with their knowledge.

## The Role of Spanking

Perhaps this is the appropriate time to discuss spanking. I am in favor of spanking, but only as a *last resort*. When something else works as well or better, by all means we should use the alternative. The difficulty is that the last resort usually comes earliest in a child's life. There is a time, very early in life, when the small child does not understand words, ideas, or instructions. Spanking may be the only way to say, "Your behavior is unacceptable," in terms the child can understand.

When the child is a bit older, other methods will achieve the desired results. Current research indicates that spanking brings positive results up to about eight years of age. After this time, spanking tends to produce resentment and has more bad effect than good. This would seem to suggest that other means of discipline should be used as the child grows older, with a gradual phasing out of spanking and replacing it with other approaches.

# Principles for Discipline

Some principles of good discipline may be helpful as "rules of thumb."

**1. The child should understand what the discipline is for and why it is being imposed.** If the child does not understand, we cannot expect improved behavior as a result of discipline. But when a child understands that what he has done is unacceptable and why the discipline is being imposed, he has a solid basis for choosing better alternatives.

**2. The discipline should be fair.** The child should get some idea of how serious the offense is by the severity of the discipline imposed. Parents should not take away a summer camping experience for some minor offense. Nor should they punish a major breach of conduct with a gentle reminder. A child learns to judge behavior by the kind of parental reaction it brings. Only through discipline that is fair can a child get a really accurate view of the way good and bad behavior fits into the world.

**3. Discipline should be consistent.** Parents reactions to their children's behavior sometimes depends on little more than the kind of day the parents have had. This standard is unfair to the child because it robs him of an opportunity to see his own behavior in clear perspective. A behavior that is unacceptable today should also be unacceptable next week. Parents should react with approximately the same level of approval or disapproval. Of course, absolute consistency is an impossibility. Parents should not worry themselves needlessly about absolute consistency. Children have a large tolerance for variation if their parents show concern for consistency even when they fail at times.

**4. Discipline should be as closely related to the offense as possible.** If a child makes a mess, the child should clean up the mess (the small child "helps" clean up the mess). If a child leaves a tool out after using it (assuming clear instructions were given about its return, of course), use of that tool may be denied for a period. If a child is unreasonably late in returning from playing at a friend's house, that friend's house might appropriately be declared off limits for a period. Or "grounding" for a few days might be an alternative.

The "Saturday box" is an idea that has worked effectively for some parents whose children leave their things scattered all over the house. Parents explain carefully to all their children that anything belonging to the child found outside the child's room will be place in the "Saturday box" and may not be retrieved by the child for use until Saturday. Some "grace" is needed early in this approach, but repeated failure to put things where they belong can be cured by depriving the child of those things for a few days.

5. ˙The discipline chosen must not harm the child. Extreme measures, even though used for centuries by some parents, are not acceptable. Measures which break bones, cut the skin, or burn or bruise the child are unacceptable. Measures which harm the child emotionally — such as locked in a closet — are unacceptable. Any measure which could be considered brutal or harsh will do more harm than good and, perhaps, inflict lasting damage.

6. Discipline should be administered by someone who loves the child and is loved by the child. A stranger cannot appropriately discipline my child. Nor can I effectively discipline someone else's child. This is not to say that a stranger should not stop a child from doing something cruel or destructive. But if discipline is to be appropriate, it needs to be administered by someone close to the child. Discipline is most effective in a context of love, support, en-

couragement, acceptance, and affirmation. In such an environment, discipline reassures the child; it says, "We love you. We care very much about you, your happiness, and your wishes. We are eager to help you have the best possible life. That is why we cannot allow you to act this way."

## Discipline of the Small Child

The small child needs close supervison and very limited freedom. He does not yet understand his world nor does he have the maturity to choose wisely. As he grows and develops, however, wise parents want him to develop independence and responsibility. These qualities develop best in an environment which allows for increasingly important choices to be made by the child.

When the child is very small and just learning, valuable and fragile objects should be placed out of reach until he is older. It is not fair to the child to expect him to know without learning. Neither is it fair to him to live in an environment in which he never has an opportunity to learn about fragile, beautiful things.

There will be some breakage; it is inevitable. But parental attitude toward it is crucial. Children should not be allowed to break things maliciously, nor should they be allowed to play in such a way that fragile things are endangered. But when breakage occurs accidentally, it is very helpful to normal growth that parents accept it without undue upset.

A small boy, who regularly helped his mother clean the dishes from the table, dropped one in the process one evening. He looked up at his mother fearing a reprimand. To his amazement his mother said, "Johnny, in all the time you have been helping me with this job I believe that is the first dish you have ever dropped. That must be some kind of record." Johnny learned that people are more important than things.

Another troublesome problem which many parents face is the temper tantrum. Parents often fail to realize that they themselves help bring on temper tantrums in their children by uncertainty in giving in to their demands. Such parents say "no" to some requests, then change to "yes" because a child persists in begging, pleading, and demanding. They are, in reality, teaching the child that he need not accept the "no," regardless of how emphatic it was when given. It is good practice to say "no" less and hold to it when said. That way occasional change for really legitimate reasons will not undermine the whole approach.

---

## "A temper tantrum is the ultimate extension of the child's demanding behavior."

---

A temper tantrum is the ultimate extension of the child's demanding behavior. Most parents feel seriously threatened by what seems like an outrageous attack on their parental authority. In their rage, they strike out at the child, spanking hard and long, and think, "This will teach the child a lesson." Sometimes this approach works, but it usually leaves scars on the parent-child relationship. The child sees a violent frightening side of the parent, which may "flash back" at times in the future in such a way as to damage the relationship. Later the parent may also have deep guilt feelings when he realizes he treated the child more severely than he would have in a more sober moment.

The better way of dealing with temper tantrums is to ignore them. Admittedly, this is difficult to do. The urge that the parent feels in such cases is, "Do something . . . anything!"

But here is the crucial consideration: who "owns" the problem, the child or the parent? If the problem is mostly "sound and fury" it's often best just to ignore it. But if the child's behavior becomes destructive — such as throwing things — it's the parent who should do something. The principle involved in either ignoring or acting is this: the child must learn that temper tantrums do not work to get one's way, nor even to get the parent's attention. Destructive behavior should carry with it, by the way, the realization that anything torn up *must* be paid for from the child's resources.

## Discipline of the Older Child

As the child approaches adolescence, we should make a gradual change in our approach to discipline. We should shift increasing responsibility to the young person by making fewer rules to restrict behavior and giving greater freedom of choice.

It is important that we keep open the lines of communication. The parents and children need to know one another's thoughts and feelings.

When an older child violates the rules, we should ask questions to find out why. Afterwards, perhaps a gentle reprimand will be enough. But when more severe measures seem to be needed, "grounding" is probably the next order. Remember, though, that involves time-consuming supervision.

"Grounding" may take several forms, depending on the seriousness of the misbehavior. For a small offense, parents might deny the young person the use of the phone for a couple of days. For a little more serious offense, they might take away visiting privileges as well: no company over or no going to the homes of friends. (Parents should be careful how they communicate this to the young person's friends who call, since embarrassment or humiliation is not part of the discipline.)

First offenses are less serious than repeated offenses. More serious offenses may be met with longer periods of "grounding." For these, parents can make some special arrangements for necessary meetings. There are times, for example, when parents must drive the young adolescent everywhere he goes. Here the rule may be that during the "grounded" period he must attend all functions in the company of parents, and may or may not be allowed to sit with friends at such functions. It can be hazardous to make sitting with parents a type of punishment. The young person should not develop negative feelings about being with his family.

## Discipline and the Mid-Teen

"Driver's license age" is an important arrival for the mid-teen. This time in his life offers increasing freedom, though not complete freedom by any means. But wise are the parents who have prepared the teenager for this new freedom in the years before it arrives.

The use of the car now adds a new dimension to "grounding." But withdrawing car privileges should probably stem only from a rather serious offense, and this only after there has been a clear understanding between parents and teenager of the nature of the offense.

The use of the car by our teenagers met with rather close restrictions during the first year of driving. This was a "learning period," and we assured each one that later they would have greater freedom.

We also tied restrictions on the use of the car to the offenses connected with driving. We were especially concerned about traffic violations. We felt that our teenagers' attitudes toward authority were being tested, so these rules were stricter the first year they had their licenses.

Most young people will respond positively to reasonable controls. It will help a great deal if the parents gradually lift the controls in the later teenage years.

## Neither Parents Nor Children Are Perfect

I believe it is an important principle of discipline (teaching) that parents be willing to allow their offspring to make some mistakes as they grow up. The principle of "logical consequences" often teaches a lesson which would never be learned otherwise.

Still, with all the best intentions in the world on the part of all parties concerned, most homes will be places where life must be lived, at least at times, in a climate of tension.

It will be helpful and reassuring to read some good books. It will also be helpful to talk to other parents.

But when parents have done the best they know to do, they can come to accept the fact that their growing teenager also must bear an increasing part of the responsibility. I like to remind parents of Psalms 89:20-24, 28, 30-34. The Lord said:

> I have found David, my servant;
>   with my holy oil I have anointed him;
> so that my hand shall ever abide with him,
>   my arm also shall strengthen him.
> The enemy shall not outwit him.
>   The wicked shall not humble him.
> I will crush his foes before him
>   and strike down those who hate him.
> My faithfulness and my steadfast love
>   shall be with him,
>   and in my name shall his horn be exalted.

My steadfast love I will keep for him for ever,
　　and my covenant will stand firm for him.

If his children forsake my law
　　and do not walk according to my ordinances,
if they violate my statutes
　　and do not keep my commandments,
then I will punish their transgression with the
rod
　　and their iniquity with scourges;
*but I will not remove from him my steadfast*
　　*love, or be false to my faithfulness.*
I will not violate my covenant,
　　or alter the word that went forth from
　　my lips.

Living with failure is occasionally inescapable.
Living through weeks or months of tension is also
necessary at times. But I believe there is every reason for parents to face the years with teenagers
optimistically.

I urge you to seek out those for whom parenting is
an exciting and immensely enjoyable experience.
Talk with these who know how fulfilling it is to help
another human being to grow toward maturity. Discover for yourself how satisfying it is to weep with
them at times and to laugh with them often. These
will become treasured memories. It is all a part of
growing up — for you as a parent, as well as for your
children!

# We Will Make It Work

## —God and the Family

### Chapter 12

Israel, God's favored people, forgot their Creator. As punishment, God allowed a generation to die in the wilderness, wandering without ever entering the promised land. God told the next generation how to avoid repeating the sins of their fathers, which crippled the nation. Moses taught them that the only hope in preserving their nation rested in how well they taught their children the law of God (Deut. 6:4-9).

In a series of speeches, Moses talks to God's people about their children and homes.

For what great nation is there that has a god so near to it as the Lord our God is to us, whenever we call upon him? And what great nation is there, that has statutes and ordinances so righeous as all this law which I set before you this day? Only take heed, and keep your soul diligently, lest you forget the things which your eyes have seen, and lest they depart from your heart all the days of your life; make them known to your children and your children's children.

Deuteronomy 4:7-9

Hear, O Israel: The Lord our God is one Lord; and you shall love the Lord your God with all your heart, and with all your soul, and with all your might. And these words which I command you this day shall be upon your heart; and you shall teach them diligently to your children, and shall talk of them when you sit in your house, and when you walk by the way, and when you lie down, and when you rise. And you shall bind them as a sign upon your hand, and they shall be as frontlets between your eyes. And you shall write them on the doorposts of your house and on your gates.

Deuteronomy 6:4-9

And when Moses had finished speaking all these words to all Israel, he said to them, "Lay to heart all the words which I enjoin upon you this day, that you may command them to your children, that they may be careful to do all the words of this law. For it is no trifle for you, but it is your life, and thereby you shall live long in the land. . . .

Deuteronomy 32:45-47

According to Moses, the family was Israel's central agent for teaching future generations. And even today, Sunday school teachers and ministers cannot substitute for teaching in the home.

Once a pagan asked a missionary, "Sir, tell me about your god." The missionary began to tell the man about Jesus, but the pagan interrupted him. "Sir, I do not wish to know about Jesus. I want to know about that god on your wrist." The missionary replied, "That is no god! It is my watch, a time piece." "But," the pagan said, "you do nothing without consulting your little god."

We follow many "little gods" today. But we cannot allow these allegiances to threaten the Christian home, God's oldest institution.

## Spending Quality Time

It takes time — lots of time every day — for families to  become all God wants them to be.

At graduation time, parents say, "It seems like only yesterday when John started school." The song "Sunrise, Sunset" from *Fiddler on the Roof* expresses the emotion a parent feels after his child has grown up so quickly. Children live with their families about seventeen years, and school activities and dating take up much of the last six years.

Because of the desire to move up in society and culture, we spend less time with children. For a son to become a "chip off the old block," the "old block" must be around to be chipped on. Some parents say they "can't find time," but they must *take* time from something they're doing that is less important than the children. It is hard to persuade fathers to spend more time with their children. If husbands would allow wives to plan more of their agenda, they might be surprised how much this would help. Most wives know their husbands far better than the husbands think. My wife has almost absolute veto power over my speaking engagements. I need her in that role to keep a better balance in our family life. A wife can see her husband's schedule more objectively.

How many hours the father spends at work each day is not as important as how many hours he *prefers* to spend there. If a father works ten hours a day, six days a week, yet is eager to get home, he can still be a godly father. But if his profession or anything else

177

fascinates him more that his family, his priorities are out of order. He should not have chosen to marry and have children. Accepting the challenge of family life requires time, but time alone means very little — there must be motivation and desire. Outside interests can draw us away from the family, unless they include or relate to the family. A newspaper columnist wrote that the more associations and committees men and women belong to, the more unhappy the marriage is.

---

## "The family is more important than a promotion, even if the husband has to find another job."

---

In business today, promotions and raises often mean moving to another location. Is it worth moving to get a few hundred dollars more? What if the family doesn't want to relocate? Does the husband's job always have priority over the family's desires? Are there times when the husband needs to turn down a promotion? I say *yes*. The family is more important than a promotion, even if the husband has to find another job. And if that happens, the family must be willing to "tighten the belt" *without complaint*!

American business seems to care less and less about the family, and there are more and more divorced executives. In many cases, divorce is encouraged in order to give the business a "full-time" employee, undistracted by family worries or interests. Furthermore, they can move him around with less hassle and cost.

In his book, *I Ain't Well – But I Sure Am Better*, Jess Laird tells of a brilliant, young executive, who decided not to accept a promotion if it meant relocating. He and his wife decided it would be too costly for the family. This unusual response caused problems for the company. Finally, the company decided that the man must either accept the promotion and relocate or resign. With some regret, the young executive resigned. His supervisor called him into his office and said, "Al, you have the guts to do what I should have done years ago, but I didn't have the courage to do it. I have position, power, and money; but I have lost my soul, my family, and my God. I envy and admire you."

A friend of mine, an excellent computer programmer, left a university position to work for IBM. After a while, he decided to become a fireman because it would be good for his family life. He took a large cut in pay, but he is now happy in his work and has more time to spend with his family and church. Some people thought he was foolish, but I admire his courage to break the "American mold" of materialism. It needs to happen more often.

In America, there seems to be four ways to achieve success: money, beauty, intelligence, and athletic ability. We are bombarded with subtle and direct temptations to worship these "gods." But Jesus never taught that these would lead to success.

## Expressing Love

**Agape.** The New Testament introduces a form of love not naturally characteristic of man. Human love is a personal desire (eros), tender affection, or family love. But Jesus created another kind of love called agape. Human love tends to be selfish ("I need you."), but agape love is "other oriented."

Agape love "turns the other cheek" and "goes the second mile." It is not like cotton candy — tasting sweet at first but quickly evaporating to leave a mess. Christian love *stays* sweet and stands by to clean up when an ugly mess occurs. Agape love is unselfish, ready to serve. It's a love that's not just something you feel; it is something you DO, then BECOME, and finally ARE.

Abraham Maslow said, "We must *understand* love; we must be able to *teach* it, *create* it, *predict* it or else the world is lost to hostility and suspicion." Agape love is the *only* form of love that can be understood, taught, created, and predicted. Perfect agape love is seen in Christ Jesus (Phil. 2:5-9; 2 Cor. 4:15; Eph. 2:4).

Only those who seek God can learn agape love. By ourselves, without God's power, agape love is impossible. For example, it is beyond man's natural ability to "Love your enemies and pray for those who persecute you" (Matt. 5:44). According to modern psychology, only a masochist would "rejoice in . . . sufferings" (Rom. 5:3)! Unnatural characteristics become natural to the Christian through supernatural power: "God's love has been poured into our hearts through the Holy Spirit which has been given to us" (Rom. 5:5).

The Christian home, with this extra dimension of love, has the best chance to be a happy home. This super quality of love makes having a family, with all its trials, worth it all.

**Acceptance.** Christian love accepts us as we are, even at our worst. Should an unmarried daughter announce to her mother that she is pregnant, a loving mother will accept the daughter *AND* the pregnancy. Christ died for us while we were sinners (Rom. 5:6-8) and accepted us in our imperfect state. Therefore, we must learn to do the same.

Sometimes the most difficult people to accept are those closest to us. If a customer chooses the wrong color, he may return or exchange the merchandise. But if our spouse does it, we say, "You ought to know better." If your neighbor's daughter takes a quarter from your coffee table, you forgive her and find a way for her to earn the quarter. But if *your* daughter takes a quarter from a neighbor's table, how do you react? — "Don't you know that stealing is wrong? You march yourself right back and apologize to the neighbors for stealing. And if I ever catch you doing that again . . . ." Actually, it's *our* ego that makes it such a big issue — "What will the neighbors think?" Our image in the community often takes priority over what is best for our children.

One of Jesus' qualities was unconditional acceptance. He could accept the prostitutes, adulterers, crippled, poor, uneducated, prejudiced, tax collectors, and even the ones who killed him. No one was too sinful for Christ to accept. This unique way of life attracted people to him. None of us have earned God's love, and few of us are even worthy of the love of our fellow man. We must learn to accept others just as Christ accepted us, no matter how unworthy.

## Being An Example

The examples set by mom and dad make a tremendous impact. The key is to model the role you desire your children to follow. Remember: "like father, like son." Admit to your children when you are wrong, ask their forgiveness, and then, get back to the task of becoming the best example you can.

The ideal husband leads his family by being a follower of Jesus, the perfect example of a loving servant/leader. The combination of a godly father and mother provides a unified harmony that inspires children to learn the role of a father and mother.

Children remember actions much longer than they remember words. My father was a man of few words, but his character is unforgettable. I never heard him curse, use a vulgar word, raise his voice, or use sarcasm. When I sin with my mouth, my father's silent testimony comes to my mind and judges me far more effectively than anything critical he might have said.

## Clarifying Goals

Victor Frankl developed an entire field of psychiatry around the concept of "meaning" to life. To have no purpose for living undermines mental health, leaving a person aimless, disoriented, and wandering. In turn, this creates frustration and anxiety. When a person sets goals and decides what is important to him, his life develops purpose. Goals must be chosen according to Hebrews 11:13-16, which tells us that God's people are not seeking a permanent home on this earth.

When I ask troubled couples about their goals and purposes, I usually get one of three responses: (1) "To raise our children successfully," (2) "To provide for our family's financial security," and (3) "We don't have any goals; we just live from one day to the next." It is good that couples want to provide intellectual, physical, and social development, plus financial security, for their families; but these goals are incomplete. For the Christian when things come undone at the seams and he comes to the end of his rope, he ties a knot and hangs on. He waits to be rescued by the arms of Jesus — the ultimate goal.

## Positive Discipline

". . . The reproofs of discipline are the way of life, to preserve you . . ." (Prov. 6:23-24). Many families do not realize that discipline makes life beautiful. Children, for example, hate piano practice. But disciplining themselves will pay off later with beautiful music. Discipline and precision do not hinder good things; they bless them. Who wants a surgeon or an auto mechanic who was not disciplined in school? "Whoever loves discipline loves knowledge, but he who hates reproof is stupid" (Prov. 12:1).

One of the differences between man and an animal is man's ability to restrain himself from abusing his freedom. But this quality does not come naturally. Self-discipline is our defense against Satan. "A man without self-control is like a city broken into and left without walls (defenses)" (Prov. 25:28). In our society and culture, it is difficult to discipline ourselves from overeating and overspending. We often wish that self-discipline would come more easily. Maybe that is why it is so highly prized by God.

The book of Proverbs frequently mentions the need for parents to discipline their children. "Discipline your son while there is hope; do not set your heart on his destruction" (Prov. 19:18). By nature children do what they *want*, not what they *ought*. So parents are told to discipline them until they can discipline themselves. The phrase "spare the rod and spoil the child" is worth remembering, but it is not an exact quote from the Bible. The text is actually much stronger: "He who spares the rod *hates* his child . . . " (Prov. 13:24). To neglect discipline is to hate the child because he will grow up without one of the qualities that makes life beautiful. Also, undisciplined children make life miserable for others. Lack of discipline is double injustice to the child himself and to mankind in general. Consider the upbringing of men like Charles Manson and Lee Harvey Oswald. In the long run, discipline is a pleasant quality. Discipline may seem "painful rather than pleasant," but disciplined people later yield the "peaceful fruit of righteousness" (Heb. 12:11).

But how much discipline? How far do you go? Most agree physical punishment doesn't work very well with teenagers. Denial of privileges works better.

183

In cases of serious discipline, husband and wife should agree and be aware of possible consequences. Be consistent. If a child violates a family rule and you promise discipline, be sure to follow through. A child does not interpret leniency as "grace," as parents often think. A child may see himself as victor. "I won that one." "By mere words a servant (or son) is not disciplined, for though he understands, he will not give heed" (Prov. 29:19). Discipline must "get his attention" or hurt in some way — or it has no effect. The action taken must be strict enough to cause the child to "think twice" when he is tempted to do the forbidden again. It is terrible for parents to be too harsh on children, but this is rare compared to the number of parents who allow their children to go unpunished when they desperately need it.

---

## "Discipline without a consistent pattern of praise has little effect in rearing children."

---

The foundation for all discipline is love. Any discipline, no matter how mild, is out of order if it is not obvious to the child that both parents love him deeply. It is almost impossible for loving parents to overdiscipline! Love disciplines only for the child's benefit, never because of the parents' impatience, resentment, or selfishness. No matter, how many rules a child breaks, parents should emphasize his good traits more than his faults. A parent must not criticize more than he compliments. Families with well-adjusted children call attention to positive things and spend as much as 90 percent of their time complimenting behavior and building up the child's self-image. They spend large amounts of energy

184

*looking* for the positive. Discipline without a consistent pattern of praise has little effect in rearing children.

## Devotional Time

Many families feel guilty if they do not have a regular devotional each evening. But I would like to relieve some of that guilt.

The traditional evening devotional time usually works well for children from the sixth grade down; but when they start junior high school, they usually start a "reversal syndrome." The adolescent phase of their life begins with a trend to move away from parents' rule and toward independence. Parents may need to loosen their hold a little, letting children "find themselves" and develop independence in their spiritual lives, too. Remember the promise: "Train up a child in the way he should go, and when he is old he will not depart from it" (Prov. 22:6).

Demanding attendance at family devotionals often works against what God emphasizes as effective methods of influencing children's lives. In addition to the "reversal syndrome," children develop strong interests outside the family. School activities increase and tend to exclude the family. Football, basketball, chorus, band, and out-of-town trips can disrupt a family schedule. Sometimes even a computer can't work out a time when all can be together for a family meal or devotional.

**The Biblical Method.** A better method is what educators today call "teachable moments," times when children are ready to learn. But long before that phrase was invented, the Bible was telling us how to create "teachable moments."

Picture a young, Jewish boy watching his family eat unleavened bread for seven days, followed by a luxurious feast. They do this regularly, year after year. One day the boy finally asks his father, "Dad, what are we doing this for?" The Jewish passover feast (Exod. 13:3-16) created fantastic curiosity. Questions came naturally, creating a "teachable moment." The father answered, ". . . It is because of what the Lord did for me when I came out of Egypt" (Exod. 13:8).

Another child asks, "Dad, what is that blood sprinkled on the door for?" (Exod. 12:7-13). Curiosity provoked the question, and the father has another opportunity to explain. On another occasion, a child sees his father kill a beautiful calf — a strange thing indeed! Questions follow "But why, Dad? If it wasn't sick, why did you kill it?" Again, the father has a teachable moment. "And when in time to come your son asks you, 'What does this mean?' you shall say to him . . ." (Exod. 13:14ff).

---

### "We need to put more emphasis today on creating teachable moments."

---

A Jewish boy walking along the Jordan River comes to a stack of plastered stones with writing on them. That evening he tells his father, "Dad, I was by the river today and saw the strangest thing." "What was it, son?" "Well, it was a stack of rocks that had been plastered together with some writing on them." "How many were there?" "Well, I think there were about twelve." Now the father recalls the history of the boy's forefathers. He explains how that stack of rocks was a memorial of thanksgiving and dedication to God for his help in their crossing the Jordan River. He tells how God helped them conquer the promised land, though they were greatly outnumbered. ". . . When your children ask

186

in time to come, 'What do those stones mean to you?' Then you shall tell them . . ." (Josh. 4:6-7).

The Israelites had many memorials, reminders, and traditions that created *spontaneous* devotionals. They were not confining or monotonous, but occurred naturally while the people sat in their houses, walked by the way, laid down, and arose (Deut. 6:7). We need to put more emphasis today on creating teachable moments. Unless curiosity is stirred, there isn't much learning. Too often, planned teaching is boring. Older children call it "forced religion."

Curiosity is still alive in the church today: "Mother, what does baptism mean?" "Yes, but why are they putting her under the water?" "Is there any other way to baptize?" "Dad, can I have some crackers and grape juice?" Too often parents say, "Hush, child, get your hand off that tray. Sit back and behave yourself." They could have said, "That's a good question. After the service I'll show you some 'crackers.' It is also called unleavened bread for a very special reason, and I will tell you why." That's the perfect time for a spontaneous devotional.

Devotionals don't have to include only prayers and Bible reading. There can be study also. Nature studies are fantastic ways to provoke curiosity, teach lessons, increase faith, and inspire devotionals. Jesus, the master teacher, often used illustrations from nature. In Matthew 6:28 he said, "Consider the lilies of the field . . . ." He also talked about birds (Matt. 6:26), seeds (Matt. 13:1-9, 24-30), sheep (Luke 15:3-7), trees (Matt. 7:16-20), grass (Matt. 6:30), moths (Matt. 6:19-20), and dogs (Matt. 7:6).

Solomon also knew how to create curiosity with nature studies. He stirs curiosity when he says: "Go to the ant . . . consider her ways and be wise"

(Prov. 6:6); "...things that are too wonderful... the way of an eagle in the sky, the way of a serpent on a rock, ..." (Prov. 30:18-19); "the badgers are a people not mighty, yet they make ..., the locusts have no king, yet all of them ..., the lizard you can take in your hands, yet it is ..." (Prov. 30:26-28).

I grew up in a home with no *formal* devotionals, but my mother *taught* me about Christ and God through nature. She pointed out the marvels of God by calling attention to the stars (Ps. 19:1-2). She sang hymns to herself and encouraged the entire family with her singing devotionals. She walked with us through the parks talking about the beauty of God's creation. Today, she still teaches me about birds' traits and habits and reminds me to "feed the sparrows" because, as she says, "God loves them just as much as he loves the blue jays and red birds" (Matt. 10:29).

There is a world of things to provoke a child's curiosity. A wise parent will begin looking for ways to conduct devotionals that seem *natural* to children, devotionals that are interesting and will make them *want* to learn more about God.

Our family has found that as each child goes to bed there is a "gentle moment" when parent and child can have a short, positive talk, ending in prayer. Some of the sweetest prayers I have ever heard came from our children during a "gentle moment." This time also serves as special, private time with each child, building strong relationships between parent and child.

## Personal Quiet Time

Parents cannot build strong families without giving God top priority each day. God must have *choice* time each day — not because he needs it but because we need it. We need him for wisdom in making decisions. We need him to balance our lives, to give us comfort and grace when things go wrong, and to encourage us when events are depressing. Everytime I foul-up and disappoint myself, I look back and see several days in which I failed to give God choice time.

An hour each day is ideal. If you need help learning how to use your time, buy Stephen Olfords' little pamphlet, *Manna in the Morning*. Also, keep a notebook of your meditations, prayers, and reflections. This spiritual diary will be a blessing in several ways. As you read back over your prayers, you will be reminded of your commitments; and you will be able to see progress. It will remind you when you miss quiet time with God, and it will help you remember some of the thrilling days with Christ in private devotion. Your motivation to live for Christ will increase. Writing things down somehow imprints them on the mind.

Make quiet time simple: read, pray, reflect. Reading the Bible first usually sets the tone for your prayers. Do not use this time for reading any other book. No book speaks more directly to your heart. Christians may read many books to maintain maturity and growth in Christ, but they must never let any other book have precedence over the book of God. You can't share the word of God spontaneously when you "walk by the way, when you lie down, and when you rise up" unless you *possess* it.

## Respect For Individual Differences

No two children are alike. Like fingerprints and snowflakes, each child is unique. We must never expect a child to have the same characteristics or abilities as big sister or big brother.

Look at your hands. Each finger is different. They don't fight each other for superiority. The "ring fin-

189

ger" doesn't reign over the other fingers because it wears the ring. The four "alike" fingers don't out-vote the thumb because it's an oddball. Each one is needed; each one is wanted. You wouldn't try to change any one of them and you are happy all the fingers cooperate as different parts of the same hand.

In comparison, each individual in the family is of equal value. No soul is worth more than any other; they are just different and have different roles. The father bears ultimate responsibility (Eph. 5:21ff). The wife has immediate responsibility under him, and the older children usually assume more respon-sibilities than the younger siblings. Also, boys have different job descriptions than girls. Each member has a different job, but all are *equally loved*.

Parents who believe that each child should be given the same privileges, same opportunities, same birthday gifts, and *everything* the same don't realize children are not exactly alike! Their sex is different; their age is different. Their maturity, per-sonality, interests, and rate of physical, mental, and spiritual growth all vary. Wise parents study each child, learn individual characteristics, and meet specific needs with an individual plan for growth in Christ.